M000190599

Mountain Biking
the Berkshires

Help Us Keep This Guide Up to Date

Every effort has been made by the author and editors to make this guide as accurate and useful as possible. However, many things can change after a guide is published—establishments close, phone numbers change, hiking trails are rerouted, facilities come under new management, and so on.

We would love to hear from you concerning your experiences with this guide and how you feel it could be improved and be kept up to date. While we may not be able to respond to all comments and suggestions, we'll take them to heart and we'll also make certain to share them with the author. Please send your comments and suggestions to the following address:

The Globe Pequot Press
Reader Response/Editorial Department
P.O. Box 480
Guilford, CT 06437

Or you may e-mail us at:

editorial@globe-pequot.com

Thanks for your input, and happy biking!

Mountain Biking the Berkshires

Anna Milkowski

FALCON®

Guilford, Connecticut
An imprint of The Globe Pequot Press

Copyright ©2001 by The Globe Pequot Press

Falcon and FalconGuide are registered trademarks of The Globe Pequot Press.

Cover photo: Index Stock Imagery

Library of Congress Cataloging-in-Publication Data

.
Milkowski, Anna.
    Mountain biking the Berkshires / Anna Milkowski
        p. cm. — (A Falcon guide)
    Includes index.
    ISBN 1-56044-769-9
        1. All terrain cycling—Massachusetts—Berkshire Hills — Guidebooks. 2. Trails — Massachusetts — Berkshire Hills — Guidebooks. 3. Berkshire Hills (Mass.) — Guidebooks. I. Title. II. Series.

GV1045.5M42 B475 2001
917.4'10444—dc21

                                                          2001023610

♻ Text pages printed on recycled paper.
Manufactured in the United States of America
First Edition/First Printing

Table of Contents

Acknowledgments vii
Map Legend viii
Area Map ix

Get Ready to Rumble! 1

How to Use this Guide 2

Being Prepared 6
    Dressing for the Occasion 7
    The Bike 7
    Tools 8
    Water and Food 8
    Company 8
    Navigation 8
    Flora and Fauna 9
    Weather 9
    First Aid 9
    When to Ride 10

Riding Right 10
    Trail Manners 10
    IMBA Rules of the Trail 11

North County 15
  1 Berlin Mountain Loop 17
  2 Mt. Greylock—Old Adams Road Loop 21
  3 Mt. Greylock—Bellows Pipe Loop 27
  4 Savoy—Bog Pond Loop 31
  5 Savoy—Downhill-Lover's Delight 34

Central County 39
  6 Cruising in Kennedy 41
  7 Kennedy Park—Aspinwall Loop 45
  8 Yokun Ridge Loop 48
  9 Rambling on East Road 52
10 Lenox Fire Tower Spur 56
11 Dean Hill Road Loop 59
12 Taconic Skyline Trail—Route 20 to Berry Pond........................62
13 Pittsfield State Forest Zigzag 67
14 The Boulders—Better than Boulder 71
15 Rolling through the Hilltowns 74
16 Windsor—Jammin' the Jambs 78

17 Ashuwillticook Rail Trail 82
18 October Mountain—Boulder Trail Loop 86
19 October Mountain—Felton Lake Loop 89
20 October Mountain—Ashley Lake Loop 92

South County 97
21 Beartown—Mt. Wilcox Road Loop 98
22 Beartown Trails Epic..101
23 Sheffield Flats Road Loop 106
24 Thousand Acre Swamp Road Loop 110
25 Mt. Washington—Ashley Hill Jaunt................................113
26 Mt. Washington—Alander Mountain................................116
27 Sandisfield Road Loop 119

Appendix 1—Resources...123

Appendix 2—Getting Involved with the Bike Community 125

Index of Rides..126

Glossary 127

Acknowledgments

Larry Gadd and Cia Elkin provided me with invaluable encouragement and guidance. What an interesting journey this turned out to be!

I began writing this book jointly with my brother, Stefan Milkowski. When he signed off as co-author and headed for other adventures, like Alaska and college, he signed on as my most-valued adviser. He and my parents, Susan Hartung and Antoni Milkowski, kept me going. "Thanks" is hardly sufficient.

A long-ago summer working at the Arcadian Shop in Lenox gave rise to the idea of this guide, and since then the Arc has supported me in numerous aspects of this endeavor. Thanks to Ken and Tom, for repeatedly resurrecting my bike, to Steve, for his advice on guidebooks, and to Larry and the rest of the crew for entertaining my incessant questions.

Thanks also to: Betsy and Max Gitter, whose interest always spurred me on; Rob Stein, Chris Leggett, and others from the ski team, who may not remember the enthusiasm they showed for this project back when it was still an idea; Sara Cushman, Eva Dienel, Molly Breen, Emer O'Dwyer, and the many friends who kept me in touch with life outside the woods; and the editors who created this book, Peggy O'Neill-McLeod, Erin Turner, and Joshua Rosenberg.

Working with Berkshire bikers and those involved with land management proved a highlight of this project. To thank a few: My riding partner Vince Conway, who generously shared wisdom and anecdotes gained in thirty-plus years of Berkshire biking; Heather and the folks at the Mountain Goat; Gloria Wesley of the Berkshire Cycling Association; Leslie Reed Evans of the Williamstown Rural Lands Foundation; Joan Allen of the Vermont Land Trust; George Wislocki of the Berkshire Natural Resources Council; Mike Downey; and Rebecca Barnes of Massachusetts DEM.

Mountain Biking the Berkshires Map Legend

Interstate		Campground	
U.S. Highway		Picnic Area	
State or Other Principal Road		Buildings	
Forest Road		Peak/Elevation	4,507 ft.
Interstate Highway		Elevation	x 4,507 ft.
Paved Road		Gate	
Gravel Road		Parking Area	
Unimproved Road		Overlook/Viewpoint	
Trail (singletrack)		Bridge	
Trailhead		Gas Lines	
Trail Marker		Power/Utility Lines	
Waterway/Waterfall		Forest Boundary	
Lake/Reservoir		Map Orientation	N
Meadow/Swamp		Scale	0 0.5 1 MILES

Berkshire County
and Surrounding Areas

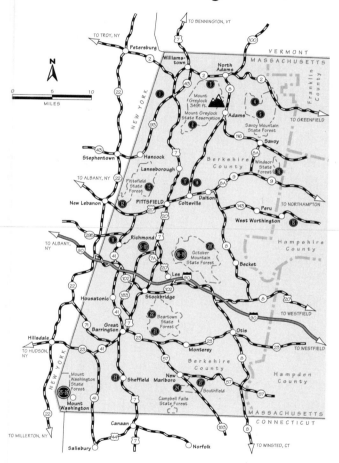

Get Ready to RUMBLE!

You're standing in a thicket, panting, gulping water that tastes like mildew, with soaking wet feet, sweat in your eyes, and thorns in your forearm—smiling. All around you, blackberries hang in grapelike bunches—so abundant and so delicious you're tempted to load them into that smelly water bottle to take home for a pie. Picking berries, feeling your legs burn after a steep climb, flying down a rocky descent, and walking your bike up the hill that's a little too steep are all part of mountain biking. Mix and match these elements to make your ride as mellow as sipping coffee over the Sunday paper or as intense as running an ultramarathon at 11,000 feet. However fast or far you go, the pleasures of the sport are yours to enjoy.

The Berkshires are well known as a natural haven just a jump from the crowded cities of Boston and New York. Rolling, wooded hills, fast-running streams, and granite mountaintops surround small towns rich in history. Clearly, there's got to be some mountain biking in them thar hills—and there is. Ridges, mountaintops, mud bogs, fir forests, autumn leaves, pastures, fields, streams, slate, shale, and granite play canvas for trails flat and steep, long and short. But for years, information on the sweetest (and sweatiest) climbs and the best picnic jaunts has passed word of mouth. Don't waste any more time cursing your friend's bad directions! We're writing this book so that Berkshire bikers have a carefully researched and transportable resource, one that accompanies them to the lobby of the dentist's office, in the passenger seat of the car, and on the bike. It's for the rider toting binoculars and a bird book, the well-shaven racer looking for a new shale cliff to descend, and the novice who's picked the bike as the key to a newly professed healthy lifestyle. Locals will cry: "And I never even knew this trail left from my own back yard!" Part-time residents may sign on full time. Those looking for a vacation spot will come here. Hundreds of miles of trails are packed into one compact county, where you can ride in the morning, feast at a country inn in the afternoon, and hear a world-class symphony by night. There's something here for you all.

How to Use This Guide

We searched out the best of Berkshire County's dirt roads, logging roads, hiking trails, and bridle paths and created a collection of rides that range from singletrack mountain climbs to smooth and flat doubletrack outings. We've even included some rides on prime dirt roads. (Scoff these off until you encounter deer fly season.) Most rides stay within Berkshire County, but a few extend into adjacent counties and states. We stayed clear of places where bicycling is prohibited or discouraged. In state forests, we stuck to trails designated for bikes even though biking is allowed on some hiking trails in some forests, figuring we'd give hikers a little peace.

Trails we include that run on private land do so legally. We won't send you tearing across anyone's lawn. Posted signs can spring up overnight, however. Always check land access, and ride only where you're welcome. So here it is: la crème de la crème.

This guide contains 27 mountain biking rides, grouped

as North County, Central County, and South County. Each write-up begins with a rundown of the ride's vital stats, so you can get a feel for its character. Write-ups will help you pick the right place for you and get the most out of it once you get there. Here's what they mean:

Ride number provides a shorthand way of identifying a ride. This number will be used to cross-reference rides.

Ride name is typically based on the name of the trail or a key geographic feature of the ride.

Location succinctly states where the ride takes place.

Distance will tell you the length of the ride, in miles.

Time gives an estimate of ride length for an intermediate rider. The time of a ride will vary greatly between riders. As you follow the first few rides in this guide, see how your ride time measures up to ours, and use this to customize your estimated travel time for future rides. Trail conditions will also greatly affect ride time. Rocks as coarse as 25-grit sandpaper most days may offer an ice-rink-with-sneakers-on feel other days.

Tread tells you whether the ride takes place on singletrack, doubletrack, dirt roads, or, gasp, paved roads. Don't rely too heavily on this as a navigational tool; sometimes the lines between treads are fuzzy, particularly between double-track trails and dirt roads.

Aerobic level describes just how much lung power the ride will require. Rides are rated easy, moderate, and strenuous.
   Easy: Flat or gently rolling terrain. Any hills will be short and gradual.

Moderate: Hilly but not grueling. Climbs will be short and steep or long and gradual. Some hills may require walking.

Strenuous: Frequent or prolonged climbs that employ the granny gear heavily. Cardiovascular fitness, fresh legs, and a gung-ho mindset make up the checklist of essentials for a strenuous ride.

Technical difficulty ranks bike-handling rigors on a scale of 1 to 5.

Level 1: Bare-bottom smooth surfaces, namely paved roads.

Level 2: Smooth with some easily avoidable obstacles. An example is a rutted dirt road.

Level 3: Irregular tread with some rough sections: rocks, roots, tricky curves, and steep sections that require nimble weight shifts. Lines will be obvious, and no leaping ability required.

Level 4: Rough riverbed terrain with few smooth places. Picking the right line will be tricky and essential through an unforgiving mass of rocks, stones, branches, ledges, and roots. Jumping ability will come in handy.

Level 5: Continuously broken, rocky, root-infested, clifflike, or trenched tread. Finding the right line will be a needle-in-the-haystack search. None of the rides in this book are rated at level 5, but sections are. These will challenge any non-Nepalese yak type to stay on the bike. Lift your front wheel up that cliff, then bunny hop onto the narrow rock strip on the right—get those legs spinning for that 20 percent grade!

Hazards: That something not-so-special: Tire-flattening broken glass, killer mosquitoes, or huge mud pits. We'll tell you here if you're sharing the trails with off-road vehicles like four-wheelers and motorcross bikes, which bring engine roars and often mud pits, unmarked trails, and litter.

Highlights: That something special: a swimming hole or a terrific view, a downhill lined with blueberries, or the quietest, most scenic, prime spot for a snack, whether you're eating a rock-hard energy bar or water crackers and fine cheeses.

Land Status: A list of managing agencies or land owners. Many of the rides in this book are found in state-run parks and forests, but some rides cross land owned by individuals, towns, and a variety of land organizations. Be aware: land status can change overnight.Always leave gates as you found them and respect the land, regardless of who owns it. Please obey all no trespassing signs and obtain permission before crossing private property. See Appendix 1 for a list of local addresses for land-managing agencies.

Maps: A list of maps covering the ride. Our map will get you through the ride, but we recommend riding with a topographic map, particularly if you intend to do any exploring. United States Geological Survey (USGS) publishes highly detailed, 7.5' (1:24,000) topographic maps stocked by most local outdoor retailers. Wildflower Productions publishes a CD-ROM version of Berkshire County topographic maps titled TOPO! The $50 price tag isn't so steep when you consider that twenty-plus quadrangles cover the county. Department of Environmental Management (DEM), the state agency that runs state forests and parks, publishes free topographic maps of state forests. In some cases, these maps include trails not on USGS maps. These same maps are often available at the state forests themselves, but just in case the Eagle Scout–built brown wooden map box is empty, we strongly recommend picking up a map in advance. You can pick up a set at DEM's regional headquarters in Pittsfield (see Appendix 1).

Access describes how to get to the trailhead, where to park if you come by car. We wanted the descriptions good, so in some cases they're long.

The ride guides you through the ride mile by mile, but keep in mind that odometer calibrations vary. Lots of great riding is packed into the Berkshires. The downside of this is that riding in some places, Kennedy Park to name one, you'll reach an intersection every tenth of a mile. Be patient. Follow a ride until you have a feel for the trails in an area, then head out and explore.

Ride maps will get you through the ride and let you know the terrain. Included on the map is key information such as where to park, where to picnic, and where to peer out at the grandest autumn vista. But stay on your toes—trails pop up and roads move. In some areas, not all trails will appear on the map, for the sake of simplicity. For rides in large and remote areas, we recommend riding with a topographic map in hand (see above).

Elevation graphs denote key vertical changes and indicate tread type and technical difficulty. Use them to prepare yourself mentally for a big climb or to get psyched for a grand downhill. Keep in mind that the graph approximates elevation changes—don't be alarmed by a little riser in a segment that appears on the graph as pure downhill.

Being Prepared

Black bears, coyotes, and rattlesnakes all make their home in Berkshire County, but the primary danger out there is failure to use common sense. Riding safely is a result of preparation and decision making that maximizes your options and allows for mishaps. Don't plan a ride, for example, that on your best day, in the best conditions, without one pit stop, would bring you home just as the sun sets. This is when you find yourself dehydrated, undernourished, riding recklessly through the dark. And then your derailleur breaks.

Dressing for the Occasion

First off, always wear a helmet. Given that many falls are broken with the hands, bike gloves are also good idea. They have saved many a palm. Bike shorts in an array of styles will see to it that you're comfortable on the saddle. Extra clothing such as a fleece jacket or a windbreaker (stay away from sweat-sopping cotton) is also essential. Even if it's 75 degrees and you're bright red and overheated, a twenty-minute break or a brisk wind can throw a chill on you. Bugs can be mind-boggling at times. If this would bother you, bring insect repellent.

The Bike

This guide is written for those on mountain bikes—fat tire, triple chain ring, and durable beasts. Beyond this, the key is not the bike you're riding, but the condition it's in and how prepared you are to respond to any deterioration of this condition. Make sure your bike is in fine shape when you head out for a ride. At the very least, check the front and rear brakes, headset, shifters, and tire pressure. If this sounds unfamiliar, get a bike mechanic to show you. Flat tires are a part of mountain biking, so learn to fix one, even if it means practicing at home.

Tools

We've all had those rides where we skimp on preparation, forgoing tools ("just this once"), then find ourselves sitting in a mug bog swarming with mosquitoes, trying to repair a flat with leaves and a Powerbar wrapper. Carry a patch kit, spare tube, pump, and Allen keys while riding. Duct tape can do almost anything. Many riders carry a chain tool, a pocketknife, and spare cables. Keep in mind, though, that tools are only useful if you know how to use them. Bike stores typically carry an abundance of succinct and useful guides to bicycle repair.

Water and Food

Always bring water, and drink it. Dehydration makes you more susceptible not only to heat-induced illness but also to hypothermia and frostbite. Bring an emergency snack, even if you're just going out for a short ride. Unexpecteds such as waiting out a thunderstorm, watching a flock of turkeys, and crossing streams can pop up and turn short rides into long ones.

Company

Ride with others, in case you or your bike suffers a debilitating mishap. If this isn't an option, be sure to tell someone where you're going and when to expect you, so he can summon help if you don't return. Many of these rides are remote! Solo riding is so potentially dangerous that if you're planning on a lot of it, consider investing in a cell phone.

Navigation

One of the obvious hazards of heading into the woods is getting lost. Know your planned route and bring a topographic map in case you have to find a way to change your route. It can never hurt to bring a compass, and whistles use less energy than shouting.

Flora and Fauna

The Berkshires offer up some environmental hazards. Watch for poison ivy and poison oak. However pristine some mountainside river looks, don't take a drink unless you have a giardia wish. Ticks carrying Lyme disease are a serious concern, so be sure to check your legs after each ride for any ticks (look closely, because the ticks are tiny) or swollen, red tick bites. Precautions considerably minimize the dangers of biking in the woods, so don't let unfounded fear keep you inside.

Weather

Following the "If you don't like the weather, wait five minutes" adage, Berkshire weather is extremely variable. Be prepared for heat, humidity, hail, blazing sun, thunderstorms, and snow squalls—all in one day. Not quite, but close.

First Aid

A small first-aid kit can come in handy when minor medical mishaps occur. Recommended items include butterfly bandages, adhesive bandages, gauze compress pads and gauze wrap, allergy pills, emergency water purification tablets, moleskin, antiseptic swabs, sunscreen, energy bar, and emergency blanket. For emergencies, stay calm and get help. There are a number of excellent books in print on emergency wilderness medicine.

When to Ride

Given our snowy winter and subsequent mud season, the Berkshire mountain biking season typically runs from May or June through October. In most state forests and parks, mountain biking trails open May 1. In notoriously muddy Savoy, don't bother to show up before June. **Call ahead to check trail conditions.** (See Appendix 1 for phone numbers.) Certain times during the summer, you may opt for dirt road rides over trail rides to stay clear of the bugs.

Hunting season is a fact of life with Berkshires mountain biking, given that hunting is allowed in all Berkshire state forests and parks. Various seasons take place throughout the spring and fall, but the big scare (since shots are taken from long range) is deer season, which typically runs mid-November through mid-December. Hunters are prohibited from firing within 500 feet of an occupied dwelling and within 150 feet of a "hard surface road" (backwoods roads don't make the cut)—restrictions that don't give much solace to a mountain biker. If you venture out, wear blaze orange, or at the very least the brightest items in your cycling wardrobe, and talk and whistle as you ride. In Massachusetts (but not in New York), hunting is prohibited on Sundays, but caution is still advised. Kennedy Park (Rides 6 and 7) and the Boulders (Ride 14) are free from hunting, and road loops are generally a safe option. Don't despair; it's time for ski season anyway!

Riding Right

Trail Manners

Respect for your surroundings is an essential element of mountain biking. We mountain bike partly to take in the sounds and sights of the wild, wild woods, so let's treat our woods nicely. You've heard it a million times: don't litter, don't be excessively loud, and try not to run over centuries-old lichens. Joining a local mountain biking organization maintaining trails is fun way to preserve our trail network and generate goodwill toward mountain bikers. (See Appendix 2.)

Respectful behavior should extend to others you encounter while riding. Yield to uphill riders. Yield to walkers. If there are horses, yield to them. It's better to respect other trail users and step aside for a minute than to have everyone mad at you and see trail access for mountain bikes taken away. When a reckless rider roars down a hiking trail, causing the hiking family to just barely haul up their three-year-olds by the shirt collars and dive to the side, we all lose. Like the finest Olympian profiled on tear-jerking up-close-and-personal TV coverage, be an ambassador for your sport!

IMBA Rules of the Trail

Thousands of miles of dirt trails have been closed to mountain bicyclists. The irresponsible riding habits of a few riders have been a factor. Do your part to maintain trail access by observing the following rules of the trail, formulated by the International Mountain Bicycling Association (IMBA). IMBA's mission is to promote environmentally sound and socially responsible mountain biking.

1. Ride on open trails only. Respect trail and road closures (ask if not sure), avoid possible trespass on private land, obtain permits and authorization as may be required. Federal wilderness areas are closed to bicycles and all other mechanized and motorized equipment. The way you ride will influence trail management decisions and policies.

2. Leave no trace. Be sensitive to the dirt beneath you. Even on open (legal) trails, you should not ride under conditions where you will leave evidence of your passing, such as on certain soils after a rain. Recognize different types of soils and trail construction; practice low-impact cycling. This also means staying on existing trails and not creating new ones. Be sure to pack out at least as much as you pack in. Some of the rides feature optional side hikes into wilderness areas. Be a low impact hiker also.

3. Control your bicycle! Inattention for even a second can cause problems. Obey all bicycle speed regulations and recommendations.

4. Always yield trail. Make known your approach well in advance. A friendly greeting (or bell) is considerate and works well; don't startle others. Show your respect when passing by, slowing to a walking pace or even stopping. Anticipate other trail users at corners and blind spots.

5. Never spook animals. All animals are startled by an unannounced approach, a sudden movement, or a loud noise. This can be dangerous for you, others, and the animals. Give animals extra room and time to adjust to you. When passing horses use special care and follow directions from the horseback riders (dismount and ask if uncertain). Chasing cattle and disturbing wildlife is a serious offense. Leave gates as you found them, or as marked.

6. Plan ahead. Know your equipment, your ability, and the area in which you are riding—and prepare accordingly. Be self-sufficient at all times, keep your equipment in good repair, and carry necessary supplies for changes in weather or other conditions. A well-executed trip is a satisfaction to you and not a burden or offense to others. Always wear a helmet.

Keep trails open by setting a good example of environmentally sound and socially responsible off-road cycling.

North County

Massachusetts's highest mountain, 3,491-foot Mt. Greylock, stands as the predominant feature of North County, looming over purple hills and Williams College's purple cows. Given this, it should come as little surprise that the scale of North County riding is large and the nature of it is hard core. The weather runs a little harsher, the rivers run a little colder, the mud season runs a little longer. This is Greylock Country.

You'll climb 1,100 feet in less than 2 miles to reach the Taconic Crest Trail (TCT), a hiking trail that runs a 35-mile north-south span, from Prosser Hollow Road in Petersburg, New York, to U.S. Route 20 in Hancock, Massachusetts. The trail is open to mountain bikes from New York Route 43 in Hancock to Petersburg Pass on New York Route 2 in Petersburg. Great views await you if you survive the climb up and handle the eroded trail and frequent navigational challenges. Posted signs on trails accessing the TCT crop up frequently, challenging locals and land management organizations to find creative solutions to preserving ways to use the trail. Do your share by never riding on posted land and by being a respectful rider, particularly given the tenuous situation on the TCT. Once you ride the trail, you'll probably agree it could use some water bars.

In Mt. Greylock State Reservation, trails designated specifically for mountain bikes (riding on hiking trails is prohibited here) are well maintained and generally well marked. Rides 2 and 3 scale the mountain's shoulder, and while they are certainly rigorous, gradual grades make them rideable to many. A visitor center offers maps, friendly chatter, a 6-foot wide 3-D map of the reservation, and a wealth of interpretive programs from bird watching to salamander spotting. A war memorial stands at the top of Mt. Greylock, which can be reached by car (or bike) on Rockwell Road. Also at the summit is Bascom Lodge, an Appalachian Mountain Club hut that houses many an Appalachian Trail through-hiker and serves a mean breakfast.

Chances are you've never had reason to go to Savoy, a spot of a town in the far-flung reaches of northeastern Berkshire County. Until now. Mammoth 11,180-acre Savoy, with 55 miles of trails, is a mountain-biking gold mine. Grab a friend, pack a lunch, make the trek, and hit the trails. Consider combining a ride with a trip to North Adams's hot ticket—Mass MOCA, a contemporary museum built in old mills and that's fast becoming one of the world's modern art meccas. You'll drive home worn out, satiated with fresh air, and amused that you ever termed the rest of the Berkshires "rural."

Berlin Mountain Loop

Location: Hancock.

Distance: 11.5-mile loop.

Time: 3 to 4 hours.

Tread: 6.3 miles on doubletrack; 4.4 miles on dirt road; 0.8 mile on paved road.

Aerobic level: Extremely strenuous—this is a mountain-climbing loop.

Technical difficulty: 4. The ascent on Mills Hollow Trail isn't extremely technical, but given the constant climbing, one unlucky bounce off a root can have you walking. The descent on Berlin Pass Trail is extremely eroded and places a high premium on picking a good line.

Hazards: Having your hands morph permanently into claws on the descent.

Highlights: Riding on the ridge with pure blue sky and gazing out at the 360-degree view from the summit of Berlin Mountain. (Consider bringing a kite!)

Land status: In Massachusetts, DEM; in New York, NY Department of Environmental Conservation.

Maps: USGS Berlin and North Adams; *Taconic Crest Trail Map,* available through the Williamstown Rural Lands Foundation; *Williams Outing Club North Berkshire Outdoor Guide* map. There is also a book specific to the TCT, *Guide to the Taconic Crest Trail,* published by the Taconic Hiking Club.

Berlin Mountain Loop

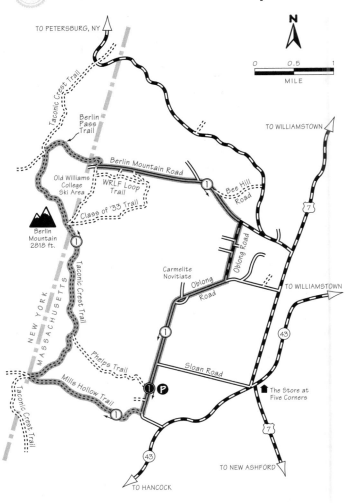

N

0   0.5   1
MILE

TO PETERSBURG, NY

Taconic Crest Trail

Berlin Pass Trail

Berlin Mountain Road

TO WILLIAMSTOWN

Old Williams College Ski Area

WRLF Loop Trail

Bee Hill Road

Class of '33 Trail

Berlin Mountain 2818 ft.

Taconic Crest Trail

NEW YORK

MASSACHUSETTS

Carmelite Novitiate

Oblong Road

Oblong Road

TO WILLIAMSTOWN

43

Phelps Trail

Mills Hollow Trail

Sloan Road

The Store at Five Corners

7

Taconic Crest Trail

43

TO HANCOCK

TO NEW ASHFORD

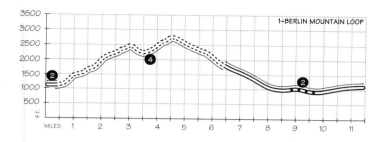

Access: From the center of Williamstown, take U.S. Route 7 south 4.1 miles to Five Corners, where Route 7 intersects New York Route 43. From Five Corners, take a right on Route 43, then an immediate right on (the fifth corner) Sloan Road. Drive 1.2 miles then take a left onto Oblong Road (dirt). After 0.3 mile, park on the right hand side of the road, at the (unmarked) trailhead for the Phelps Trail.

The ride

- **0.0** Head south on Oblong Road.
- **0.4** On your right take note of a red gate. Ignore it! Proceed 50 feet further to a gravel road, Mills Hollow Trail, and turn right, going directly across (in a direction perpendicular to Oblong Road) an agricultural field.
- **0.5** Once you have crossed the field, follow the blue-blazed trail as it enters the woods and heads left along the field edge.
- **0.6** Bear right.
- **0.7** Turn right, up a steep hill. The climb begins here.
- **1.2** A huge barren spot created by logging marks the only time during the climb where for a few seconds you can get away without peddling. Then it's back to more rubbly ascending!

19

2.0 You finally made it! Turn right onto the Taconic Crest Trail, which is marked by white pyramid-shaped blazes. Mountain biking is allowed in this section of the TCT.

2.3 Qu'est-ce que c'est que ça? More steep uphill!

2.4 Raspberry fields forever. Indulge and forget about all that climbing.

2.6 A steep tenth of a mile.

2.7 Down a wooded section.

2.8 Phelps Trail descends on the right. Stay your course.

3.1 Some hard-earned descending.

4.5 Tear off your supplemental oxygen tanks—you've reached the summit of Berlin Mountain! Enjoy the view from this flat grassy spot. Find Mt. Greylock to the southeast. A white scar on the side marks a recent landslide in the part of the mountain called "The Hopper." Clockwise from Greylock: At two o'clock is Jiminy Peak Ski Area streaked with trails; at five o'clock is the Albany skyline (on a clear day); and at eight o'clock is Vermont's Glastonbury Mountain. Behind Albany the ridgelines of the Catskills and the Appalachian Mountains can be seen. The Hoosac range sits at nine o'clock. In the fall, hawks migrate past the summit. Bring your jacket and your binoculars for an autumn double-decker of both foliage and fauna.

4.5 On the eastern side of the summit, a trailhead marks the way to an old ski trail. This is not an advisable shortcut. Head down the mountain on the TCT, which continues straight from the way you came.

4.8 See a red jeep on the right, a monstrosity easier to take if you consider it pop art, not litter.

4.9 A white-blazed trail merges in on the left.

5.1 Other side trails enter. Each time, stay to the right.

5.7 Take a right on the Berlin Pass Trail.

6.1 Despite boulder-moving efforts, ORVs reign in this section and have created eroded trails and large mud pits that should be avoided at all costs, as they are the swallowing kind.

6.7 The trail pops out on Berlin Mountain Road. Follow the road to the right to the former Williams College Ski Area (0.1 mile away).

6.8 Turn around and head down the road.

8.1 A road merges in from the left.

8.3 Bee Hill Road, in this section an overgrown double-track trail, veers off to the left and climbs north to Massachusetts Route 2; continue straight.

8.9 The dirt road joins a paved road. Take a right onto Oblong Road (instead of heading straight, across a bridge).

9.7 Take a right (still Oblong Road, though now incarnated as dirt), watching for huge houses with great views. There's even a purple house (on the left).

11.2 Cross Sloan Road.

11.5 Back at car.

Mt. Greylock— Old Adams Road Loop

Location: New Ashford.

Distance: 8.2-mile loop.

Time: 1 to 2 hours.

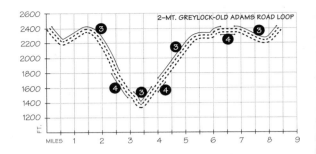

Tread: 8.2 miles of doubletrack.

Aerobic level: Moderate. Cheshire Harbor Trail climbs gradually for a solid mile.

Technical difficulty: 3 to 4. Old Adams Road and Cheshire Harbor Trails are smooth. You won't be doing much sightseeing riding the lower section of Red Gate, though.

Hazards: Newly cut tree stumps on the Red Gate logging road bypass.

Highlights: Fast cruising on Old Adams Road. Raspberries galore in midsummer. Finding a good climbing rhythm up Cheshire Harbor Trail.

Land status: Mt. Greylock State Reservation (DEM).

Maps: USGS Cheshire; DEM Mount Greylock State Reservation and Greylock Glen.

Access: From Park Square in Pittsfield, take U.S. Route 7 north toward Williamstown. After 6.7 miles, turn right on North Main Street in Lanesboro, following brown signs to the Mt. Greylock visitors center. Bear right onto Quarry road after 0.8 mile. After another 0.4 mile, bear left on Rockwell Road. In another 0.6 mile, the Mt. Greylock visitors center stands on your right. After securing some useful maps at the center, wind up Rockwell Road for 3.8 miles to the large dirt parking lot on your right. The lot is known as the "Jone's Nose" lot, after a hiking trail by that name. In the lot, a tiered collection of wooden signs points to the various trails.

The ride

0.0   From the signs, head down Old Adams Road Mountain Bicycle Trail, the doubletrack at the far end of the parking lot. The trail cruises easily, at times as smooth as a drag strip.

0.5   Take a left (not a 90-degree right onto an anonymous trail that descends to Cheshire).
After 200 feet, take a left again, following a wooden sign that points you toward Old Adams Road.

1.1   Obstacles become more frequent.

1.4   Cross the Appalachian Trail. In June or July you may catch a resting through-hiker here, gathering energy to climb 1,000 feet up Saddleball Mountain on the way to Greylock.

1.5   Take a right on the doubletrack trail at the T intersection. This is Red Gate Trail, marked only by plastic placards put up by snowmobilers.

1.6-1.8 The trail's narrowing coincides neatly with a pricker patch. Great. This portion can also get fairly muddy.

2.1   A logging skid road heads left. Continue straight, over a decrepit palette bridge.

2.2   The trail levels, then becomes a short, narrow descent. At the bottom, a logging road goes left. Continue straight.

2.4   Turn right onto the logging trail that Ts in from the right. This is the beginning of a 0.3-mile bypass of an unrideable section of the Red Gate Trail. If you miss

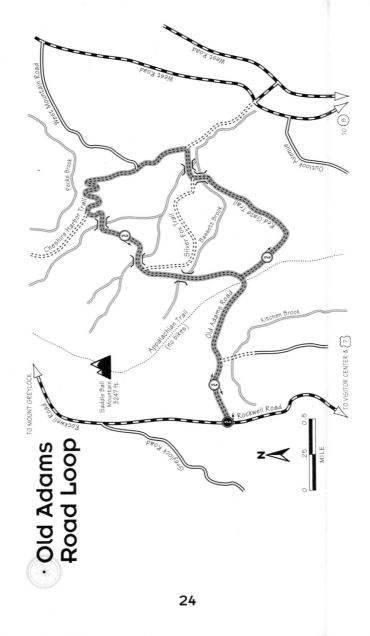

Old Adams Road Loop

West Road

West Road

West Mountain Road

Pecks Brook

Cheshire Harbor Trail

Silver Fox Trail

Bassett Brook

Red Gate Trail

Outlook Avenue

TO ⑧

Old Adams Road

Kitchen Brook

TO VISITOR CENTER & ⑦

Appalachian Trail
(no bikes)

Saddle Ball
Mountain
3247 ft.

TO MOUNT GREYLOCK

Rockwell Road

Greylock Road

Rockwell Road

N

0   .25   .5
MILE

this turn, in less than a tenth of a mile Red Gate Trail becomes a chute of rocks, branches, leaves, and fallen trees.

2.5 The trail levels in what appears to be the center of this logging operation—a wide-open spot with abundant stumps and fallen trees. From here, the ride becomes a rocky descent. Keep an eye out for small stumps lurking under dried leaves.

2.7 The bypass rejoins the Red Gate Trail. Five feet downhill from where the trails merge, a stone, 2-foot-high rectangular marker stands on the left. A little farther downhill (less than 0.1 mile), if you happen to notice, is a grassy trail heading left as you pick your way down the descent; don't turn onto it. Also ignore the grassy trail that veers in from the right. Prepare for the next rocky 0.1 mile.

3.0 A steep, wet hillside descends on your left. The trail, though lacking turns, has plenty of rocks, leaves, tree segments, and even some rotting carpet to keep things exciting.

3.1 Enjoy a brief flat spot, then turn left across an old wooden bridge.

3.2 Just across the bridge, turn right and cross another. Cruise down a grassy doubletrack enclosed by green cover; the noisy stream is on your right.

3.4 At the top of a rise, the trail Ts into West Mountain Road (a doubletrack). Take a hairpin left.

3.6 Intriguing light spots a ravine on the left. Climb over a flurry of water bars.

3.7 A trail enters from right.

3.8 Ascend a rocky section.

3.9 Climb up to a large dirt parking area. Head out in the same trajectory as you entered, into the field and then bend left, following the sign to Cheshire Harbor Mountain Bicycle Trail.

4.0 Ride around a white-striped brown gate, heading uphill. Try to find a rhythm early on for this mile-long climb. A set of switchbacks will let you know you're nearing the top. Side trails cut between the switchbacks—don't let them confuse you.

5.0 Old Adams Road intersects Cheshire Harbor Trail on the left. Turn left, grateful you're not heading up this rock-strewn section of Cheshire Harbor. (This section of Cheshire Harbor Trail, from Old Adams Road to Rockwell Road, the paved road to the summit of Greylock, makes a roaring fun descent, particularly if you are well suspended. Climbing it is less fun.)

5.1 Cross a bridge.

5.7 Cross a bridge and the rock section around it, then enter land of many ferns.

6.0 Ride up that tricky uphill section.

6.1 Cross a bridge, then a rocky and wet patch that can be difficult.

6.7 Your friend Red Gate merges in from the left.

7.6 Turn right and head uphill.

8.0 Raspberries in July.

8.2 Return to the parking lot.

Mt. Greylock— Bellows Pipe Loop

Location: North Adams, Adams.

Distance: 13.6-mile loop.

Time: 1.5 to 2.5 hours.

Tread: 7.7 miles on doubletrack; 4.8 miles on dirt road; 0.9 mile on paved road; 0.2 mile after-dinner mint of single-track.

Aerobic level: Strenuous.

Technical difficulty: 4. Expect some steep and rocky sections.

Hazards: Rumor has it this trail can get pretty windy, hence the Bellows Pipe name. On West Mountain Road, watch for ORVs. Keep an eye on the sky too, because you're

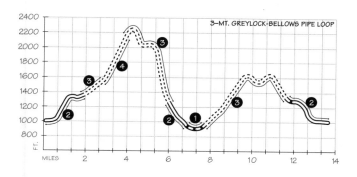

riding on the side of the highest peak in Massachusetts, 3,491-foot (scoff away, Westerners) Mt. Greylock.

Highlights: Climbing gradually along a riverside on a cared-for and quiet trail, hammering home up the most fun "paved" road ever.

Land status: Mt. Greylock State Reservation (DEM).

Maps: USGS North Adams; DEM Mt. Greylock State Reservation and Greylock Glen; *Williams Outing Club North Berkshire Outdoor Guide* map.

Access: From the junction of Massachusetts Route 2 and Massachusetts Route 43 in Williamstown, head east on Route 2 for 1.2 miles. Turn right onto Luce Road, which soon becomes Pattison Road. At 3.2 miles from the junction of Route 2 and Route 43, park at the trailhead for the Appalachian Trail.

The ride

0.0 Follow Pattison Road east. A reservoir providing water to North Adams is on the right. Check your own bottle cages or desert-animal hydration system for a fat quantity of water—you'll need it. If empty, go directly to jail. (Do not pass Go.)

0.8 Bear right onto Notch Road.

1.9 Just past the intersection with Reservoir Road, turn left onto the Bellows Pipe Trail, a welcoming, wooded doubletrack.

2.8 Dance up a steep section for 0.2 mile.

3.5 Charge up another tricky part.

3.9 Cross a stream, then shoot up a steep hill. (Pattern here?) Take your pick, left or right. Left is a little less steep.

· Bellows Pipe Loop

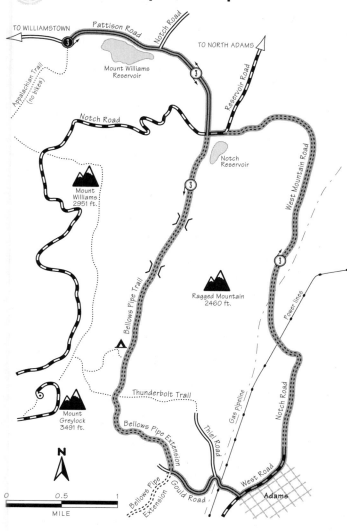

4.2	Level ground! Breathe a sigh of relief.
4.4	Just past the Bellows Pipe Shelter, a hiking trail goes uphill to the right to reach the Appalachian Trail. Stay left on the Bellows Pipe Trail, following the sign that reads TO THUNDERBOLT TRAIL TO THIEL AND GOULD ROADS VIA MOUNTAIN BIKE TRAIL. The descent begins tamely, growing fiercer as you pick up speed.
4.7	Cross the Thunderbolt Trail, a hiking trail.
5.0	Bear left as a trail merges on the right.
5.3	Bear right. Check out the view of Adams.
5.5	Bear left onto a singletrack.
5.7	Take a left when you pop out onto Gould Road (dirt). Greylock Glen, currently another prime mountain biking destination, but slated for development, is on your left.
6.4	Turn right onto Thiel Road (dirt).
6.7	Turn left onto West Road (paved).
7.2	Bear left onto Notch Road (paved).
7.4	This paved road begins its demise with an innocuous ROAD UNDER CONSTRUCTION sign. Incline increases proportionally with the amount of rubble in the road.
8.5	Cross under a power line.
8.6	Ignore the side trails on the left, and the rest to follow. Explore these at your own risk. You may get lost, and you may be trespassing.
9.0	Cross a gas pipeline.
9.6	By golly, at long last, the top!
10.2	More up! Hang in there, it's only two-tenths of a mile.
10.7	Bear right just past a collapsed house on your left.
11.3	Stay straight, instead of taking a 90-degree right down a technical-looking trail.
11.5	Pavement! Take the left option, up the steep hill. Lucky for that granny ring.

11.7 You have circled around to the Bellows Pipe trail-head. Turn right onto Notch Road, the way you came in.

12.6 Bear left.

13.6 You have completed the loop.

Savoy—Bog Pond Loop

Location: Savoy.

Distance: 3.6-mile loop.

Time: 0.5 to 1 hour.

Tread: 2.4 miles on dirt road, 1.2 miles on doubletrack.

Aerobic level: Easy.

Technical difficulty: 2 to 3.

Hazards: Forgetting to call ahead for a mud report and finding yourself in the midst of a mosquito breeding frenzy.

Highlights: A little doubletrack, a little dirt road, a few itty-bitty uphills, a few itty-bitty downhills, ledge here,

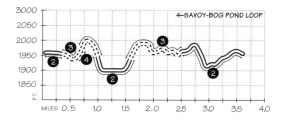

loose rubble there, and still time to read a chapter of a novel at Bog Pond and energy enough for a fine swim at North Pond.

Land status: Savoy Mountain State Forest (DEM).

Maps: USGS North Adams; DEM Savoy Mountain State Forest.

Access: From the junction of Massachusetts Route 8 and Massachusetts Route 2 in North Adams, head east on Route 2. Drive 5.2 miles and turn right onto Central Shaft Road. Follow this road 3.4 miles to the North Pond parking area.

The ride

0.0   From the southern end of the parking lot, head south on the dirt road (Florida Road).

0.4   Turn left onto Haskins Trail, following a sign that reads TRAIL TO BOG POND. This wide, leaf-softened trail cruises through the woods. Huge water bars and the occasional rock shelf provide a chance to practice nimbleness.

0.7   Bog Pond Trail, a skinny hiking trail, Ts in from the right. Continue straight up the rocky hill.

1.0   The trail pops you out onto New State Road. Take a right.

1.2   A road leading to Black Bear Farm goes left. Try to catch a glimpse of the grazing llamas. Savoy has it all!

1.3   Bog Pond comes into view on your right. A hiking trail follows the shore, accessing sheltered picnic spots.

1.6   Take a right turn on Carpenter Trail, which crosses the road. The trail rolls easily.

2.4   Take a right onto Florida Road, and ride back up to your parking spot.

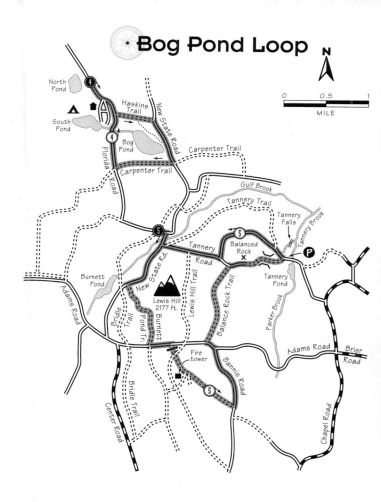

3.6 You're back at North Pond. The pond bottom is spiked with sharp rocks, but the water is gloriously refreshing.

Savoy—
Downhill-Lover's Delight

Location: Savoy.

Distance: 8.2-mile loop.

Time: 1.25 to 2.0 hours.

Tread: 3.8 miles of doubletrack; 4.1 miles of dirt road; 0.3 miles of paved road.

Aerobic level: Moderate. This ride maximizes downhill fun by climbing on roads and descending on trails.

Technical difficulty: 3 to 4.

Hazards: Extreme mud (don't even think about coming before June), bugs, ORVs, and scarcity of people.

Highlights: Sweeping around the banked hairpins of Balance Rock Trail, watching hawks at Burnett Pond.

Land status: Savoy Mountain State Forest (DEM).

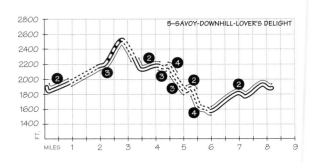

Maps: USGS Cheshire; DEM Savoy Mountain State Forest.

Access: From the junction of Massachusetts Route 2 and Massachusetts Route 116 in Adams, head east on Route 116 7.4 miles. Take a left onto Center Road. Drive 2.9 miles and take a left onto Adams Road. After another 0.2 mile, turn right onto New State Road. Then, drive 1.5 miles and take a left, and then an immediate right into the parking lot.

The ride

0.0 Turn left out of parking lot. After a few hundred feet, at the first intersection, turn right onto New State Road (dirt), and ride down a hill and over a bridge.

0.2 Tannery Road (dirt) Ts in from the left. Continue straight.

0.9 It's worth a trip down the gated trail to Burnett Pond on the right. When you return from the pond (the way you came), take the trail directly across the road. This is Burnett Pond Trail. You'll coast over moss and needles through a dark moist forest where silence pervades. A short section is narrow and deep from erosion, leaving only roots and rocks sticking up but for most of the time you can concentrate on the scenery instead of the terrain.

1.8 The trail turns into terrible, wet shape. Go right at this muddy junction, and within 0.1 mile you'll pop out onto Adams Road (dirt). Take a left.

2.2 Take a right where a gated paved road turns uphill. A side trail on the right dodges the gate. Here begins the climb to the top of Borden Mountain—not technical except for a few eroded patches, but sufficiently long and steep.

2.3 Kamick Trail goes right. Continue climbing on the road.

· Downhill-Lover's Delight

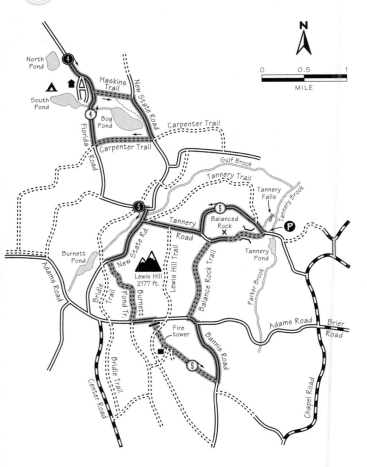

2.5   At the top of the hill is an old fire tower, unusual among local fire towers since it lacks posted signs and gates forbidding climbing it. If you can't help yourself, climb away, just be mindful of rotting wooden steps falling apart under your weight. Up top, where the height is dizzying and the wind ferocious, peer out at Mt. Greylock and the Catskills.

2.6   Take the leftmost turn onto Fire Tower Trail, and head downhill. Wide, gradual, dry, fast but not mean (few rocks!), the trail is a marriage counselor for rider and mountain bike, sending you over smooth, unexpected jumps.

3.3   Turn left onto Bannis Road (dirt).

4.0   Turn left onto Adams Road (dirt).

4.1   Turn right onto Balance Rock Trail. The trail descends smoothly, for now.

4.4–4.7   First rocks, then mud make for excitement.

5.0   Another tricky section, just in case you wanted to get any momentum for the impending hill.

5.1   The trail Ts into a dirt road. Take a right, up a steep hill. (To cut the ride short, take a left here, ride the 0.2 mile to Tannery Road, take a left and skip to mile 7.3 of this description.)

5.2   Balanced Rock, a big boulder resting on a surprisingly small base, comes into view on the left. The narrow doubletrack trail on the right is yours, but first ride over and check out the rock. If the Fire Tower Trail hasn't satiated your appetite for turning, this trail will. The newly cut doubletrack twists through trees, over bumps, zigzagging across a swath of hurricane-torn trees. Recycled rubber water bars fold magically under your front tire. Wow.

5.4   Transitions. Transitions. Transitions. A steep down. A sharp left turn. A steep up.

5.7   And again, a steep down, then a swing up.

6.2 The trail bends right, across a bridge

6.3 The trail Ts into Tannery Road. Here you have the option of taking a 0.4-mile round-trip side tour to Tannery Falls, Savoy's waterfall. To head to the falls, take a left onto Tannery Road and an immediate (10 feet) right into a parking area. After about 100 feet, take the red-blazed trail down to the left. The tricky (4 and 5) singletrack trail parallels the river and ends at the falls. Having spent the ride avoiding Savoy's notorious mud pits, the falls give reason to appreciate Savoy's mass quantities of water. Exit the falls the way you came, then turn right on Tannery Road (dirt).

6.8 Tannery Trail begins on the right; stay on the road.

7.3 Pass Balance Rock Road on your left.

7.7 Lewis Hill Ts from left; continue straight.

8.1 Turn right onto New State Road, familiar terrain. Cross the bridge, climb up the short hill, and take a left on Burnett Road.

8.2 Turn right into the parking lot. Hopefully the bears haven't gotten to your car.

Central County

Central County, the section that's home to the most people in Berkshire County, is also home to the most riding.

Tiny Kennedy Park, one-tenth the size of most state forests, is the hub of Central County mountain biking. This small town park, with trails both flat and hilly, straight and lugelike, welcomes riders of all abilities. (Turn to Ride 6 for your first-ever mountain bike ride, Ride 7 for singletrack thrills.) The town of Lenox manages the park superbly. Trails are well marked and some intersections even have trail maps posted. Water bars are built to keep trails dry, gravel fill is spread on muddy sections to prevent erosion, and fallen trees are quickly cleared so trails stay narrow. No motorized vehicles are allowed. Instead, sports teams train on the trails, dogs take their owners for walks, and hikers picnic in a gazebo. Kennedy is also the launching point for a host of other rides on the Yokun Ridge. Rides 8 (a hilly ride with some great singletrack), 9 (a mellow, scenic mix of doubletrack and dirt roads), and 10 (a hard-core climb with a super technical final pitch) can all be accessed through Kennedy Park.

The Taconic Skyline Trail (Ride 12) has its own unique virtues and flaws. Once you climb up to the trail from U.S. Route 20, the riding is fast and fun, with tricky ups and downs thrown in for variety. When you're sick of riding tons of little loops, the feeling of going somewhere is exhilarating. On the downside, you half expect to come across a gang of escaped convicts at the Route 20 trailhead, and even if some ORVs don't roar by, you will feel their presence. Huge mud pits, extreme trail erosion, and a good dose of litter are all part of the ride. This is still a great ride, and if you want more, you can follow the trail north from Berry Pond in Pittsfield State Forest all the way to the top of Jiminy Peak Ski Area. Pittsfield State Forest is also home to Ride 13, a hill-climber's favorite. You will climb up a mountainside, go down it, then climb up and go down it again.

The Boulders in Dalton (Ride 14) is Pittsfield's version of Kennedy Park—a friendly, well-used, unmotorized place too small and with too few trails to get seriously lost in. Graffiti on The Boulders alludes to the land's less illustrious past as a headquarters for underage drinking.

Beginners and experts alike should also head to Windsor State Forest (Ride 16)—a fantastic treasure trove of easy trail and dirt road riding. You'll pass through spectacular spruce forests that look nothing like the rest of the Berkshires. Call ahead for a mud report here, and don't be surprised to see a bear scamper off.

Three nontechnical rides will bolster any rider's aerobic capacity. The Ashuwillticook Rail-Trail (Ride 17) is so flat you will barely shift. Rolling though the Hilltowns (Ride 15) and Dean Hill Road Loop (Ride 11) require more finger dexterity.

Eleven thousand-acre October Mountain State Forest is a bear. Foul weather, mud, a proliferation of unmarked trails, and the scarcity of people can make this place scary. Bring friends! Rides 18, 19, and 20 provide three entries to the forest's massive cache of technical riding. Boulder Trail and Felton Lake Loop will keep you agile and can be paired into a single ride. Ashley Lake Loop is a faster ride—a virtue when October's voracious bugs are in season.

Cruising in Kennedy

Location: Lenox.

Distance: 4.3-mile loop.

Time: 0.5 to 1 hour.

Tread: 2.7 miles of doubletrack; 1.5 miles of singletrack.

Aerobic level: Easy.

Technical difficulty: 3. This ride makes a great bare-bones introduction to mountain biking.

Hazards: Rounding a corner into the mouth of a horse.

Highlights: Dancing over an obstacle-strewn uphill you doubted you could, breathing in crisp autumn air in a forest of turned foliage, and chatting with friendly walkers.

Land status: Kennedy Park (town of Lenox).

Maps: USGS Pittsfield West, Stockbridge; park maps available for free at the trailside bike store, the Arcadian Shop.

Access: From the intersection of U.S. Route 7 and Massachusetts Route 7A north of Lenox, drive 0.4 mile north. Turn left into the parking lot of the Arcadian Shop.

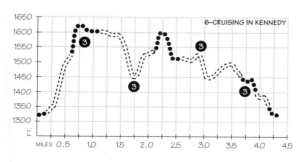

The ride

0.0 From the northwest corner of the parking lot, follow the singletrack that heads west, ever so gently uphill.

0.2 Reach a four-way intersection with a big billboard welcoming you to Kennedy Park.
Continue straight up the Overview Trail.

0.6 At the four-way intersection, turn right on Patrick Weaver Olympic Trail (formerly known as Summit Trail), named after a hometown cross-county skier who raced at Nagano. The rocky uphill is only as long as it looks.

0.8 At the six-way intersection, turn right, onto Aspinwall Trail.

0.9 Turn left on Nose as Aspinwall bears right as a black diamond descent.

1.1 You're back at the six-way intersection. Take a right onto Patrick Weaver Olympic Trail.

1.2 Let the brakes loose and enjoy a freewheeling gradual downhill.

1.4 The trail turns to singletrack. Stay left as Vagabond veers right.

1.5 Turn left onto Main Trail, a gradual and nontechnical doubletrack down. Watch for the pond on your right. The benches are a good spot for a rest, but you wouldn't want to swim in this froggy pond.

1.6 Pondside Trail heads right; stay on Main Trail.

1.8 Crest a short gravel uphill to arrive at the intersection with Overview Trail, marked with benches and signs directing you to the Lenox House Shops. Stay right on the doubletrack Main Trail, heading up a gradual rise.

2.0 Turn left on the singletrack Overlook Trail. The rocks on the trail pose the biggest technical challenge of the ride.

2.1 Reach the open-air gazebo, perched high in the park at 1,555 feet. The gazebo has benches and a ther-

· Cruising in Kennedy

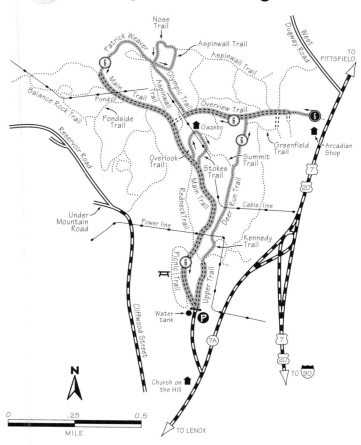

mometer. Markings identify visible peaks. Leaving the gazebo, turn left onto the singletrack Lookout Trail and pass through a thicket of burrs. Black and red raspberries reward you on the other side.

2.2 Stay right on Patrick Weaver Olympic Trail as Lookout veers left.

2.3 Just past a bouncy singletrack downhill, make a right on Stokes Trail, which curves to the right, up a short gradual hill.

2.4 The trail becomes doubletrack.

2.5 Turn left onto Main Trail.

2.6 After a small descent, cross Upper Trail. Continue straight on Main Trail, a gradual, nontechnical uphill.

2.7 Cross under power lines.

2.8 Cross through a four-way intersection and head up an eroded paved road.

2.9 At the top of the hill, turn right onto the spur to a great lookout. The place cries picnic, with soaring birds, picnic tables, wildflowers, an expansive lawn, and its open vista of the Berkshire skyline dotted with farms. Back on the trail, as you descend watch out for places where huge chunks of pavement are missing and can send you hurtling.

3.1 When you see the fence in front of you, make a hairpin left onto a trail of crumbling pavement.

3.3 At the four-way intersection (with a bench), bear right, continuing on Main Trail up a gradual, somewhat technical doubletrack.

3.5 Bear right onto Upper Trail, down a gradual downhill.

3.6 Upper Trail veers into Deer Run Trail.

3.7 Stay right as Summit Trail goes off to the left. You're heading into the most technical section of this trail, a gravely patch followed by a sharp right turn around a boulder.

3.9 Stay left as Greenfield descends on the right. At the intersection with Overview Trail, turn right.

4.1 Pass the Kennedy Park Billboard and continue straight.

4.3 You're back at the parking lot.

Kennedy Park—
Aspinwall Loop

Location: Lenox.

Distance: 4.8-mile loop.

Time: 0.75 to 1.25 hours.

Tread: 3.6 miles of singletrack; 1.2 miles of doubletrack.

Aerobic level: Moderate. Kennedy Park still wears a friendly grin no matter how tough it tries to be.

Technical difficulty: 3 to 4.

Hazards: Hairpin turns, roller-coaster singletrack, unpredictable terrain.

Highlights: Hairpin turns, roller-coaster singletrack, unpredictable terrain.

Land status: Kennedy Park (town of Lenox).

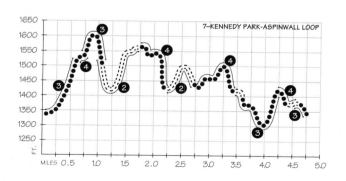

45

Maps: USGS Pittsfield West, Stockbridge; park maps available for free at the trailside bike store, the Arcadian Shop.

Access: From the intersection of U.S. Route 7 and Massachusetts Route 7A north of Lenox, go 0.4 mile north. Turn left into the parking lot of the Arcadian Shop.

The ride

0.0 From the northwest corner of the parking lot, follow the singletrack that heads west, ever so gently uphill.

0.2 Reach a four-way intersection with a billboard welcoming you to Kennedy Park. Just past the sign, turn right onto Aspinwall Trail and begin gaining potential energy.

0.6 A steep little pitch—be delicate.

0.8 Turn left at the intersection with Nose Trail.

0.9 Wowsers! A six-way intersection. Take the second left (Aspinwall Trail), descending a staircase of moss-covered rocks with a low roof of evergreens.

1.1 Wing a hairpin right onto Main Trail.

1.7 Take a left onto Balance Rock Trail.

1.8 Kirchner Trail curves left, downhill. Bear right, taking a moment to check out the 50-foot spur on the right to the illustrious Balance Rock. Check out the view of the swamp.

1.9 Bear right at the Y, through a bump that feels like an alpine ski racer's starting gate.

2.1 Turn left on Pondside Trail. The descent consists of swoosh, swoosh—a right, then a hairpin left, then smooth hard-packed singletrack out to the Main Trail.

2.3 Take a right onto Main Trail.

2.7 Veer right onto the roller-coaster Red Neck.

3.0 Take a right at the four-way intersection, then an immediate right onto Picnic Trail.

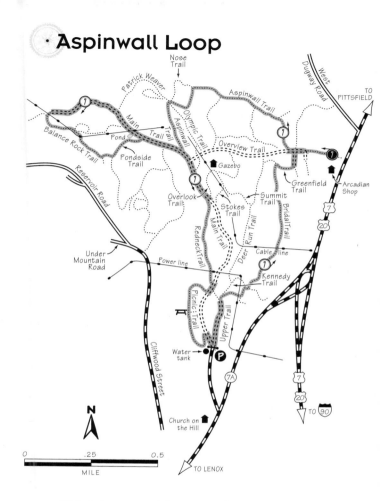

· Aspinwall Loop

This brings you right up to a huge grassy picnic area. You packed a Frisbee in that tool kit, right?

3.5 Turn right on Main Trail.
3.6 Turn left on Upper Trail.
3.7 Turn right on Kennedy Trail.

3.8 Don't cruise along that power line too fast, or you will miss the 90-degree left turn onto Bridal Trail.

3.85 Take another left.

4.4 Ride down a huge dip and across a wooden bridge. Carry your speed and you'll coast right up.

4.5 Turn left at the four-way intersection.

4.6 Turn right at the Kennedy Park billboard.

4.8 Home again, home again, jigglety-jig.

Yokun Ridge Loop

Location: Lenox.

Distance: 5.2-mile loop.

Time: 0.75 to 1.5 hours.

Tread: 2.7 miles of doubletrack; 2.0 miles of singletrack; 0.5 mile of paved road.

Aerobic level: Moderate to strenuous.

Technical difficulty: Primarily 3, with some sections of 4.

Hazards: Shooting straight into the woods on a surprise singletrack hairpin.

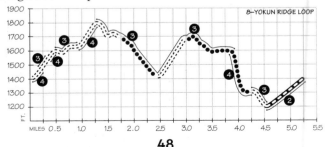

48

Highlights: Genuine skinny singletrack with tight turns, unpredictable rolling terrain, and plenty of peace and quiet. There's also a good sustained uphill to get your RDA of cardiovascular rigor.

Land status: Berkshire Natural Resources Council, Town of Lenox Water Supply. Yokun Ridge, which runs north-south from Bousquet ski area in Pittsfield to Interstate 90 in West Stockbridge, stands as a land conservation success story, where the multitude of property owners have committed themselves to land preservation. Please respect people's private property in this area!

Maps: Berkshire Natural Resources Council Yokun Ridge Map, available free at local bike shops; USGS Stockbridge.

Access: From the intersection of Massachusetts Route 7A and Massachusetts Route 183 in Lenox, head west on Route 183. After 1.6 miles, bear right onto Lenox Road. After another 1.5 miles, turn left into the parking lot at Olivia's Overlook, a lookout above the Stockbridge Bowl. A brown metal sign reads WELCOME TO THE YOKUN RIDGE FOREST RESERVATION and notes that the trails are maintained by volunteers.

The ride

0.0 Enter the trailhead directly across Lenox Road from the overlook. This is the Burbank Trail, marked by red blazes. Up, down, up . . . get used to the rolling nature of this climb.

0.1 A trail merges in from the left.

0.2 Cross underneath power lines.

0.4 Dodge roots as you ascend. A coaster downhill awaits you on the other side, then, as you bend around the corner, another uphill spurt.

0.7 Ride on up a steep section with rocks and roots, then enjoy a rest.

·Yokun Ridge Loop

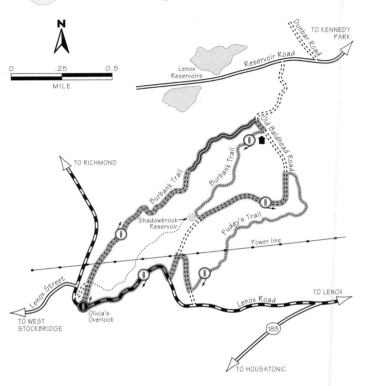

1.0 One last steep section.

1.2 A spur leads to a view of green hillsides to the left. Now you have a small rest in a descent.

1.6 The trail Ts into a wide and eroded trail. Left will take you out to Reservoir Road (0.4 mile) (see Rides 9 and 10). Take the right downhill, following the sign to Old Baldhead Road.

1.65 The foundation of an old house rests on the right side of the trail, and a plaque reads "John Gorman Homesite 1838–1898." Slow down for this, so you won't miss your trail.

1.7 Take a hairpin right onto singletrack Burbank Trail, which wiggles gently downhill.

2.3 Cross an old car-width cement bridge with funky hand railings. On your left is the Shadowbrook Reservoir, a.k.a. Monks Pond. Financier Anson Phelps Stokes built the pond in the 1890s as a means to generate electricity for his nearby 100-room "cottage." Cruise along the grass strip beside the reservoir.

2.5 Take a left on Old Baldhead Road, a smooth wide doubletrack that climbs steadily. Don't be confused by a sign reading BURBANK TRAIL that points left up the road. After about 10 feet, the trail forks. Bear right; the left is a spur along the edge of the reservoir. Baldhead Mountain is just north and east of the road. The name of this wooded peak alludes to past times when the ridge was heavily farmed.

3.0 The road levels. Veer right onto the fern-filled singletrack known as Pudgy's Trail, which joins Old Baldhead Road at a 45-degree angle. The trail twists along the side of Baldhead Mountain, offering big roots, sharp curves, and unexpected ups to keep you alert.

3.9 Cross under power lines. A steep downhill section follows. If you can't make it down without extensive brake use, walk since this section is fast eroding.

4.3 T into a doubletrack trail. Take a right, up an ever-so-slight hill.

4.5 The trail turns left under the power line corridor and follows it briefly before T-ing into Old Baldhead Road, where you turn left.

4.7 Turn right onto Lenox Road (paved). One last uphill, and a worthy one at that. Stay close to the shoulder here, as drivers unfamiliar with this curvy road frequently veer into the wrong lane.

5.2 You're back at Olivia's Overlook.

Rambling on East Road

Location: Lenox.

Distance: 11.2-mile loop.

Time: 1.25 to 2 hours.

Tread: 7.2 miles on dirt road; 3.2 miles on doubletrack; 0.8 mile on singletrack; and a touch on paved road.

Aerobic level: Moderate. The ride is mostly cruising, but these dirt roads boast some surprisingly steep sections.

Technical difficulty: 2 and 3. Technical ease is one of this ride's great virtues.

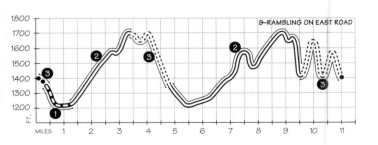

Hazards: The rare car making full use of the road around a blind corner.

Highlights: Can we say pastoral? Enjoy fast, curvy dirt road descents?

Land status: Kennedy Park (town of Lenox), town roads in Lenox and Richmond.

Maps: USGS Stockbridge, Pittsfield West; Kennedy Park maps available at the nearby bike store, the Arcadian Shop.

Access: From the intersection of U.S. Route 7 and Massachusetts Route 7A north of Lenox, drive 0.4 mile north. Turn left into the parking lot of the Arcadian Shop.

The ride

0.0 From the northwest corner of the parking lot, follow the singletrack that heads west, ever so gently uphill.

0.2 Reach a four-way intersection with a big billboard welcoming you to Kennedy Park.
Turn right just a few feet before the sign onto the Cold Spring Trail, a cool downhill singletrack.

0.5 Turn left onto West Dugway Road. Don't worry, the pavement won't last long! We find the on-road approach to the fire tower the best way to get your legs warmed up for some climbing.

1.1 Turn left onto West Mountain Road, a dirt road.

1.9 Pass Pleasant Valley Audubon Sanctuary on the right. Stop in for a hike or to learn about local birds.

2.4 Turn right onto Reservoir Road. Jaunt right up that steep!

3.2 Turn onto the doubletrack trailhead on the right, marked by boulders forming a narrow gate. Follow this trail, Dunbar Road, straight, past several right turns, gradually downhill.

·Rambling on East Road

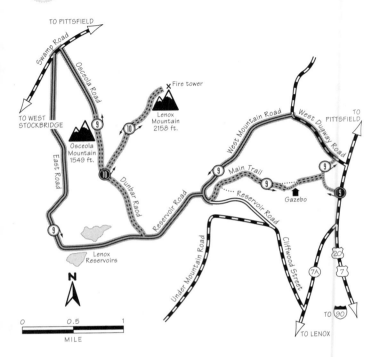

4.2 Immediately beyond a huge pile of cut-up logs, the trail arrives at the bottom of a U-shaped trail. The right-hand bend heads up to the Lenox Fire Tower, a no-holds-barred challenge for the mightiest (see Ride 10). For this ride, take the left-hand bend (still Dunbar Road).

4.9 The doubletrack turns into a dirt road, called Osceola Road, complete with cul-de-sacs and other touches of suburbia.

5.5 Take a left on Swamp Road, a paved road. Take an immediate left onto East Road (dirt).

7.3 Take a left onto Reservoir Road. Oh, the joy of a smooth descent!

8.0 Cruise between two water reservoirs. Sorry, no swimming. Get ready for an uphill.

8.6 Pass the point where you turned onto Dunbar Road back at mile 3.2.

9.4 Bear right where West Mountain Road enters on the left. Tap those brakes and swing a left onto a doubletrack trail immediately beyond a red fire hydrant. What's a fire hydrant doing out here? After 15 feet, bear right onto a singletrack that joins the Main Trail in Kennedy Park after about 30 feet.

9.7 Bear left on the Main Trail where Balance Rock Trail enters on the right. You'll ride Main Trail for the next 0.9 mile.

10.4 At the benches, continue straight (not left). Here's a fun and quick detour to the gazebo.

10.6 In the middle of a gradual climb, swing a hairpin left onto the Lookout Trail. Follow this to Kennedy's oh-so-cute gazebo, a small wooden structure with a thermometer tacked to its entrance. This place is a must in autumn.

10.7 Double back 30 feet and take a right through a wall of boulders. After you descend this fast roller-coaster downhill (into a four-way junction) you will understand how it used to be a ski jump.

10.8 At the bottom of the ski jump, take a right onto Overview Trail for the final descent. This trail is prime hiker and dog territory, so check your speed.

11.0 You're back at the Kennedy Park sign. Go straight.

11.2 You're home. (Or at the parking lot, at least.)

Lenox Fire Tower Spur

Location: Lenox.

Distance: 2.5-mile out-and-back.

Time: 0.75 to 1 hour.

Tread: Doubletrack . . . or is that streambed?

Aerobic level: Strenuous plus.

Technical difficulty: 3 to 5. If you spend your free time jumping your bike up onto picnic tables, if you feel you are the long-lost child of Evel Knievel, or if you simply like a challenge and don't mind a little hiking, you'll love this trail.

Hazards: Motorcycles, rainbow-colored oil slicks in deep puddles, extremely steep and rocky hills.

Highlights: Bathing in a purifying sweat as you test your agility; dropping your jaw at the view from the top; cliff-jumping on your way down. You deserve to feel like a hotshot if you become one of the few, the proud, to have ever ridden the entire climb.

Land status: Town of Lenox.

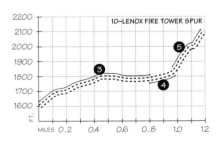

Maps: Berkshire Natural Resources Council Yokun Ridge Map, available free at local bike shops; USGS Pittsfield West.

Access: The ride begins at mile 4.2 of Ride 9. For a shorter ride, it's possible to drive to mile 3.2 of Ride 9. From where Massachusetts Route 7A merges with U.S. Route 7 north of Lenox, go north on Route 7. After 0.6 mile, just past the Arcadian Shop, turn left on West Dugway Road. After another 2.1 miles, turn right onto Reservoir Road. After another 0.8 mile, park on the side of the road; the doubletrack trail is marked by a row of boulders. Ride your bike 1 mile up the doubletrack.

The ride

0.0   Immediately beyond a huge pile of cut-up logs, the trail joins a U-shaped trail. Take the bend to the right side. Here begins the gradual climb.

0.4   I thought I was climbing! What's this downhill?

0.7   At the Y, go right.

0.8   The steep part begins. This is where a friend of ours, who has since taken up meditation and yoga, used to throw his bike into the woods, and then, fuming swears and threatening his bike with no lube for a month, hike to the top. Stay calm. Enjoy the challenge. If you don't ride up this today, there's always tomorrow. Take note of particularly steep shelves of slate and exceptionally protruding roots in preparation for your descent.

1.2   The summit! Sprawl on the grass, enjoy the view, and stay off that rickety tower! Five trails circle the tower, but the Ledges Trail, though it may sound nice, is an Audubon Trail and bikes aren't allowed, and the others shoot you right into private property and perhaps a full-body cast.

Lenox Fire Tower Spur

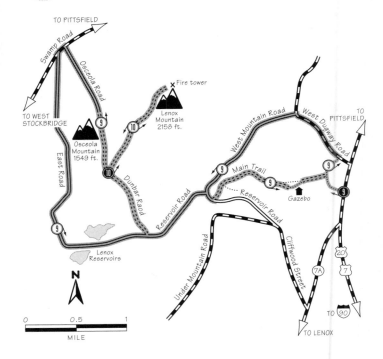

1.2 Post-picnic, turn around and head down the way you came. Put on your thinking cap (over your helmet), and exhibit some caution.

1.5 Bear left.

2.5 Back to that great pile of logs. Head home or resume following Ride 9 at mile 4.2.

Dean Hill Road Loop

Location: Richmond.

Distance: 8.6-mile figure eight.

Time: 0.75 to 1.5 hours.

Tread: 7.5 miles on dirt road; 1.1 miles on paved road.

Aerobic level: Strenuous.

Technical difficulty: Primarily 2, with a stretch of 3.

Hazards: Mud season, cars.

Highlights: Cruising fast dirt roads around corners and up and down huge hills. A stunning autumn ride.

Land status: Town roads.

Maps: USGS Pittsfield West, Stockbridge.

Access: From the junction of Massachusetts Route 41 and New York Route 295 in Richmond, head west on Route 295. After 0.6 mile, just as you crest a small hill, turn into the dirt pullout on the left side of the road.

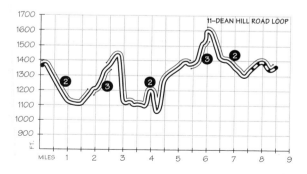

The ride

0.0 From the parking area, turn left (west) onto Route 295.

0.1 Turn left on West Road (dirt).

1.0 Take a right turn onto Rossiter Road.

1.5 The road begins climbing.

1.7 A driveway bears off to the right, ending incentive for road maintenance. Bear left, up the hill and around the right-hand bend as the road begins to disintegrate. Soon you will be climbing on a road with a solid grass strip up the middle.

2.2 Turn left when you T into a more well-traveled dirt road (Cunningham Hill Road).

2.4 Top of Dean Hill Road Ts into Cunningham Hill Road from the left. Continue straight.

2.6 A mambo downhill begins.

3.1 Cunningham Hill Road meets Miller Road in a three-way junction with a heavily foliated triangular island. Take a left on Miller Road.

3.4 Amazingly, there's even more downhill!

3.9 Take a left on Dean Hill Road. Here the climbing begins, steeply at first, then more gradually. Flower gardens line the road and edges of lawns, and open space extends to the east.

4.6 The steepest part of the hill is behind you.

5.5 Take a left on Top of Dean Hill Road, a less smooth dirt road.

6.0 At the crest, the sky is bigger than usual where a pair of scenic farm fields hug the road.

6.5 Turn right on Cunningham Hill Road. (You've been here before.)

· Dean Hill Road Loop

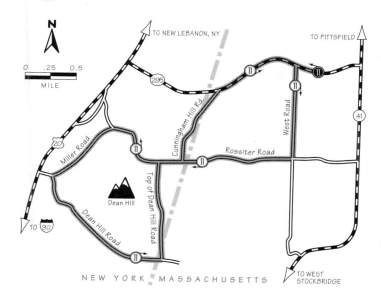

6.7 At the intersection of Cunningham Hill Road and Rossiter Road, bear left (downhill) on Cunningham Hill Road.

7.6 Take a right on Route 295. A sign immediately welcomes you back to Massachusetts. One uphill to go!

8.3 Hilltop Orchards, a great autumn apple-picking venue, is on the hill on your left.

8.4 On the left, a shingled hutch covers an old spring. Many used to get their drinking water from here, but the source has been condemned.

8.6 Back to the car.

Taconic Skyline Trail— Route 20 to Berry Pond

Location: Hancock to Pittsfield.

Distance: 9.1-mile point-to-point with shuttle.

Time: 2 to 4 hours.

Tread: 8.3 miles on doubletrack; 0.5 mile on paved road; 0.3 mile on dirt road.

Aerobic level: Moderate.

Technical difficulty: 3 and 4.

Hazards: Gasping in a breath of ORV exhaust that causes you to lose your balance and fall into a mud pit topped with green slime.

Highlights: Cruising fast flats, speeding up technical hills that occur infrequently enough for you to remain enthusiastic about them.

Land Status: Pittsfield State Forest (DEM)

Maps: USGS Pittsfield West, Stephentown Center; DEM Pittsfield State Forest.

Access: From the intersection of U.S. Route 7 and U.S. Route 20 in Pittsfield, go west on Route 20 4.1 miles and turn right on Forthill/Hungerford Road. Drive 2.4 miles and then turn left onto West Street. Shortly after, turn right onto Churchill Street, following state forest signs. The forest is on Cascade Street, 4 miles from Route 20. Drive past the guard gate at the forest entrance, turn left, and drive 0.2 mile to the left-hand parking lot. Leave car one here. In car two, drive out to Route 20 the way you came. Take a right on Route 20. After 2.5 miles, just past where the road crests Lebanon Mountain (but prior to the New York state line), turn into the paved rest area on the right. Numerous small trails scurry up the slope beside the rest area, but the main trailhead for the Taconic Skyline Trail is located about 10 feet east of the parking area.

The ride

0.0 Head up the gradual incline on the wide doubletrack trail. After about 50 feet, Griffen Trail veers right. Bear left and climb; the parking area is down a slope on your left.

0.2–0.4 Welcome to Skyline's large shale sheets and loose scree! The abundance of cliffs in this section might mean that you'd be faster hiking, but riding is more fun. Don't despair, the first half-mile of this ride is the toughest.

0.5 Welcome to the Skyline's side-trail phenomenon. The left fork is less eroded than the right. The two rejoin in 0.03 mile.

0.6 The trail levels, then descends easily. Keep alert for the third key characteristic of Skyline riding: bike-swallowing, ORV-created, frog-breeding mud pits.

· Route 20 to Berry Pond

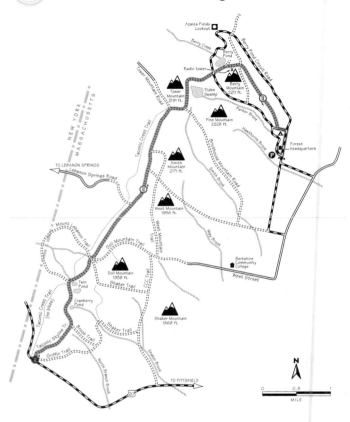

0.9 A well-worn doubletrack leaves from the right (Brook Trail).
1.4 A mud-dodging side trail enters from right.
1.6 Cranberry Pond sits through the trees on your right.
1.7, 1.8 Large mud pits. Seek higher ground!

1.9 The first pool of Twin Pond becomes visible on the right. A hiking-only section of the Taconic Crest Trail, marked by white diamond blazes, merges in from the left.

2.0 Pass beside the other pond. The next tenth is a technical uphill, but over the top lies fast flat cruising.

2.4 Descend over rubble.

2.5 A trail goes left (Lebanon Mountain Trail). Immediately after, a wet trail enters from the right (an old incarnation of Shaker Trail).

2.6 At a big dirt opening with a lone charred tree in the middle, a good-looking trail (Doll Mountain Trail) Ts on the right. Continue straight. Charge up this next hill. Stay on the main route as two grassy trails leave on the left in the next 0.2 mile.

3.8 Keep your speed on this technical down, challenging yourself to peer down at the swamp on your right. A trail Ts in from the left.

4.0 A big trail Ts from the left (Lebanon Springs Road). By now you have mastered these rubble uphills. Here's a 0.3-mile one.

4.4 A plaid couch sits beneath a tree on the left. Just past this, a well-traveled trail leaves from the right, with a snowmobile placard sign that reads TO CASCADE STREET. This is the Old Telephone Trail, which accesses Cascade Street by trespassing through some very-posted property, so continue straight.

4.7 A trail enters from the right (West Mountain Trail).

5.0 Just over a crest, the remnant of a trail enters from the right.

5.6 As the trail bends right, downhill, a trail merges in from the left (Tower Mountain Road).

5.8 Bear left around an eroded, banked, uphill corner. At the crux of the curve, a trail goes right (Brickhouse Mountain Road).

6.0 A hiking trail leaves from the right. The first trail sign of the ride (you're nearing civilization!) tells you the trail goes to Tilden Swamp.

6.1 Tilden Swamp comes into view on the right, and another hiking trail descends to it.

6.3 A right-hand side trail skirts the original trail, now a shale cliff.

6.4 Two tailgates decorate a mud pit.

6.6 A trail descends from the right.

6.8 The trail Ts into the paved Berry Pond Circuit Road. If you're up to it, take a left, riding cautiously as you proceed the wrong way on a one-way road. Berry Pond is 0.1 mile; a lookout is 0.2 mile, and the forest's famed wild azalea fields, the largest in Massachusetts, which bloom in early June, are 0.3 mile away. When you feel like heading down, you have several options. The rocky Turner Trail—bliss for the fully-suspended, misery for the rigid-framers, and a combination of the two for front-shockers—is described below. You can also take Berry Pond Circuit Road, which shoots you out at the parking lot at the forest's main entrance in 1.9 miles. Cross Berry Pond Circuit Road onto the wide dirt road.

6.9 A left fork leads to the campsites; bear right.

7.0 Turn left onto the Skyline Trail, just as the road becomes rougher and steeper. The Skyline Trail continues down as an eroded gully with side trails all over.

7.3 As the Skyline Trail bends left, North Branch Trail (marked with a wooden sign), turns right. Stay on the Skyline Trail. Just ahead, turn right on Turner Trail, also marked.

7.5 The trail, doubletrack in its truest sense, rises and follows along a short grassy ridge with sky on either side. This picturesque scene is about to end.

7.6	Rocks, roots, and leaves define the terrain. All that's left of much-needed water bars are rows of spiked rocks.
7.8	The trail gets meaner still. ("What did I do?")
8.0	The trail takes mercy.
8.3	Pass straight through a four-way intersection.
8.4	A trail merges in from the left.
8.5	Turn left on a dirt road.
8.6	Turn right on a paved road (Cascade Street).
9.1	Just before the guard gate, turn right and into the parking lot. Hopefully you remembered your car keys.

Pittsfield State Forest Zigzag

Location: Pittsfield State Forest.

Distance: 9-mile loop.

Time: 2 hours.

Tread: 8.8 miles on doubletrack; 0.2 mile on paved road.

Aerobic level: Strenuous. Some EPO sure would help.

Technical difficulty: 4.

Hazards: Off-road vehicles on the Skyline Trail.

Highlights: Huffing your way up striking mountainside trails; discovering that your kidneys are still intact after descending the Daniels Trail.

Land status: Pittsfield State Forest (DEM).

Maps: USGS Pittsfield West, Stephentown Center; DEM Pittsfield State Forest.

Access: From the intersection of U.S. Route 7 and U.S. Route 20 in Pittsfield, go west on Route 20 4.1 miles and turn right on Forthill/Hungerford Road. Make a left on West Street after 2.4 miles, then a right on Churchill Street shortly after, following state forest signs. The forest is on Cascade Street, 4 miles from Route 20. Drive 0.5 mile to the parking area at the bottom of Lulu Brook.

The ride

0.0   From the parking lot, follow Berry Pond Circuit Road uphill.

0.1   Take a right onto doubletrack Honwee Loop Trail. Take an immediate left onto the western fork of the trail.

1.6   At the fork, bear left.

1.7   Bear left.

1.8   Take a right.

1.9   Turn right on the Skyline Trail. Ears up for motors.

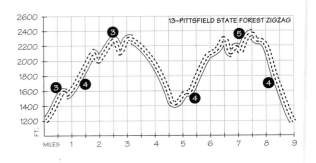

Pittsfield State Forest
Zigzag

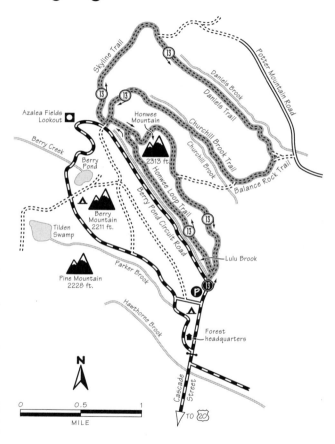

Azalea Fields Lookout

Berry Creek

Berry Pond

Skyline Trail

Honwee Mountain

2313 ft.

Daniels Brook

Daniels Trail

Potter Mountain Road

Churchill Brook Trail

Churchill Brook

Balance Rock Trail

Honwee Loop Trail

Berry Pond Circuit Road

Berry Mountain
2211 ft.

Tilden Swamp

Pine Mountain
2228 ft.

Parker Brook

Lulu Brook

Hawthorne Brook

Forest headquarters

Cascade Street

TO 20

N

0   0.5   1
MILE

3.1 Take a right on Daniels Trail. Downhill-lovers will be in heaven. This descent requires not a single turn of the pedals, but it's far from boring. Jarring rocks, high roots, rutted turns, and whatever else lurks beneath the trough of fallen leaves will keep you alert. To ease your rattled kidneys, keep an eye out for a turnout over Daniels Brook. Below, water rushes from a pool through a deep split in jagged shelves of rock.

4.7 Take a right onto Balance Rock Trail. By this point your numb body welcomes climbing.

5.1 Turn right onto Churchill Brook Trail and continue to climb.

6.4 Bear left.

6.8 Turn left onto Honwee Connector.

6.9 Go left on Honwee Loop Trail. Here begins the steep climb up to the ridge of Honwee Mountain. Stay to the right when another turnoff leads to Churchill Brook Trail. You're almost done climbing.

7.4 The flat ridge shortly turns to steep downhill, and the descent poses different challenges, such as jumping hidden water bars and dodging spiky rocks. Traction is a hope and not a guarantee, and some sections are uncontrollable. Only near the bottom does the trail allow you to ease up on the death grip and let loose for a little speedy cruising.

7.8 Bear right on Honwee, if you happen to notice the trail on your left as you descend.

8.9 Take a left on Berry Pond Circuit Road. Watch out, you're heading the wrong way on a one-way road for this tenth of a mile.

9.0 Back to parking lot.

The Boulders— Better than Boulder

Location: Dalton.

Distance: 5.7-mile loop.

Time: 0.5 to 1 hour.

Tread: 4.7 miles on doubletrack; 1 mile on dirt road.

Aerobic level: Easy.

Technical difficulty: 2 and 3.

Hazards: Foregoing all preparation—tools, clothing, food—because you underestimated The Boulders.

Highlights: Cruising easy trails and waving at joggers and hikers, your mind unburdened by concerns of the Big Bad Wolf and ORVs. Pittsfield and Dalton locals, this place is so convenient you can ride it before breakfast!

Land status: Crane & Company (the company that makes the paper money is printed on).

Maps: Crane & Company map of The Boulders; USGS Pittsfield East.

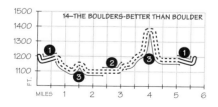

Access: From the junction of Massachusetts Routes 8 and 9 in Coltsville, head north on Route 8. After 1.8 miles, turn right on Gulf Road (dirt). This turn is hard to notice, hidden between two restaurants, Huts Pub & Grill and Pasta's Wood Fired Pizza. Drive 1.4 miles on Gulf Road to a dirt parking lot with Appalachian Trail signs on the left side of the road.

The ride

0.0 From the parking lot, turn right (west) onto Gulf Road.

0.2 Pass a gate on the left.

0.3 Pass Green Gate on the left.

0.4 Turn left on the Grey Trail, marked by grey wooden blocks nailed to trailside trees. Early rocks turn to smooth going.

0.6 Turn left on the Red Trail, a downhill coast.

1.3 Turn left on the Green Trail and cruise though a valley of ferns. Follow the blazes as you neglect two left turns in the next two-tenths of a mile.

1.8 A steep little uphill may surprise you.

1.9 Listen for frogs croaking in the swampy area on your right.

2.1 The Red Trail merges in on the right. Keep riding, and in another 50 feet follow the Red Trail as it turns right and becomes laden with roots.

2.4 A transformer structure on the right. The trail merges into a road that bends left.

2.5 Just past swampy Crane Pond (on the right), go straight, not left.

2.6 Bear right on the Red Trail as another trail goes left.

3.1 T into the Blue Trail. Go right.

3.2 Continue straight on the Blue Trail as the Red Trail leaves on the right. This next section is the toughest

· The Boulders—
Better than Boulder

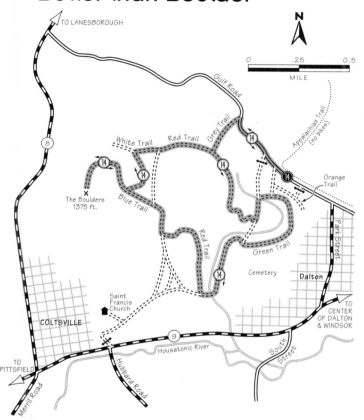

part of the ride. You're going up, and the trail is covered with lots of loose rock.

3.6 Boulders, but not "The Boulders," on right. Continue riding as the trail bends left.

3.8 The trail splits, but both forks lead to the same place.

3.9 The Boulders, covered in graffiti. Climb on, and look for a view of Pittsfield and its northerly neighboring hills, then turn around.

4.3 Turn left on the White Trail, quite narrow at the trailhead. This marks the most exciting descent yet.

4.7 Turn left on the Red Trail.

5.1 Turn left on the Grey Trail.

5.3 Turn right on Gulf Road.

5.7 Return to parking area.

Rolling through the Hilltowns

Location: Worthington.

Distance: 21.7-mile loop.

Time: 2.5 to 4 hours.

Tread: 14.9 miles on dirt road; 6.3 miles on paved road; 0.5 mile on doubletrack.

Aerobic level: Moderate.

Technical difficulty: 2, with one level 3 downhill.

Hazards: Thinking an on-road ride means you'll pass a convenience store that sells water and energy bars.

Highlights: Lounging at a swimming hole positioned midway through this rural ride.

Land status: Town roads.

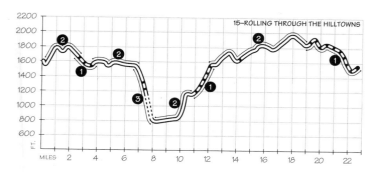

Maps: USGS Pittsfield East, Goshen.

Access: From the junction of Massachusetts Route 8 and Massachusetts Route 9 in Dalton, drive east on the then-combined Route 8 and Route 9. After 2.3 miles, turn right on Route 8. When you reach Hinsdale, drive another 3.6 miles, turn left on Massachusetts Route 143. After another 11.9 miles, park at the intersection of Route 143 and Lindsay Hill Road (dirt).

The ride

0.0 Head east on Lindsay Hill Road, into the woods.

0.2 A hill welcomes you to the ride.

2.0 To the left is Hickory Hill Ski Touring Center, the site of my first cross-country ski race. A field expands on the right.

2.1 Turn right on Ridge Road (paved).

2.6 Golf course on either side. Perhaps this is Tiger's secret training ground.

3.1 Take a sharp right on Starkweather Hill Road (paved).

3.6 Turn left on West Street (dirt).

4.1 Cross Sam Hill Road (dirt).

·Rolling through the Hilltowns

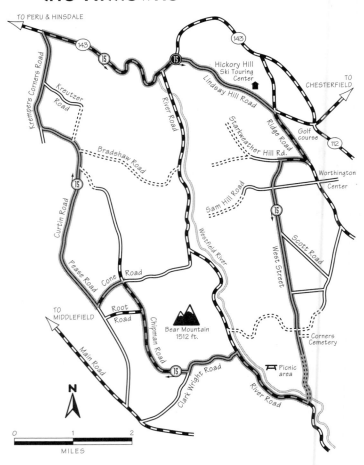

TO PERU & HINSDALE

143

15

Krempers Corners Road

Kreutzer Road

Bradshaw Road

River Road

15

143

15

Hickory Hill Ski Touring Center

Lindsay Hill Road

Starkweather Hill Rd.

Ridge Road

Golf course

TO CHESTERFIELD

112

Worthington Center

Sam Hill Road

Curtin Road

Pease Road

Cone Road

Root Road

Chipman Road

Westfield River

15

West Street

Scott Road

TO MIDDLEFIELD

Bear Mountain 1512 ft.

Main Road

Clark Wright Road

15

Corners Cemetery

Picnic area

River Road

N

0   1   2
MILES

4.8 Continue straight as Scott Road veers left.

6.0 An unmarked road (Curtis Road) Ts in from left.

6.7 Johnson Road Ts in from left; an unnamed road joins on the right.

6.9 Benjamin Cemetery Road, a short dead end to an old cemetery, leaves from the left.

7.0 The road becomes paved, but its smoothness is short-lived.

7.3 The road appears to T into another, but really this is just a sharp bend. Go left (not onto the posted road to the right). Within 0.3 mile, the pavement turns to rubble, made exciting by the steep (for a road) downhill grade.

8.1 The road regains its composure and crosses two bridges. Take a right after the second, onto River Road, which follows a healthy stream.

9.2 Welcome to Middlefield, incorporated in 1783. Just past the sign, on the right, is a riverside picnic area on with a big fire pit, numerous chairs and benches, and even a sandy beach.

9.9 Just before a cement bridge stamped with the date 1990 (make a rubbing of this historical vestige), go left onto Clark Wright Road (dirt).

11.0 Take a right up Chipman Road (paved).

11.2 The road turns to dirt.

12.6 Root Road Ts in from left. Chipman Road becomes paved at this section.

12.7 The road returns to dirt.

13.3 Arrive at a four-way intersection with Cone Road (dirt). Turn left.

13.9 Cross a bridge; the road turns paved.

14.0 Turn right onto Pease Road (dirt), and begin to climb. Stone walls hug the road on either side. An old red barn has few other buildings to keep it company.

17.0 A doubletrack trail leaves from the right (Bradshaw Road). After 0.2 mile, another doubletrack leaves on the right (Kreutzer Road).

17.8 A private road merges in from left. Signs identify the spot as Tremper's Corners.

18.7 Kreutzer Road, now a real dirt road, Ts in on right.

19.7 Turn right on Route 143. Almost all of the next 2 paved miles are downhill. Spin your legs out and relax.

21.7 Back at the gas-powered bike rack.

Windsor— Jammin' the Jambs

Location: Windsor.

Distance: 5-mile loop.

Time: 0.75 to 1.25 hours.

Tread: 3.7 miles on doubletrack; 1.3 miles on dirt road.

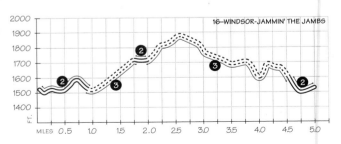

Aerobic level: Easy.

Technical difficulty: 2 and 3.

Hazards: Roads and trails are poorly marked, and don't expect to encounter much human company. The ride includes one creativity-requiring stream crossing.

Highlights: Seeing only emerald as you ride through a spruce forest dripping with moss.

Land status: Windsor State Forest (DEM).

Maps: USGS Cheshire, Ashfield; DEM Windsor State Forest.

Access: From the junction of Massachusetts Routes 7 and 9 in Pittsfield, take Route 9 to West Cummington. Turn left on River Road, following signs for Windsor State Forest. Park at the Windsor Jambs parking lot. Before you start the ride, take a tenth of a mile hike down to the Windsor Jambs, this small 1,626-acre state forest's showcase item. Water cascades through a chasm of 80-foot granite cliffs out of which rugged evergreens miraculously grow.

The ride

0.0 From the parking lot, turn left (west) onto Schoolhouse Road.

0.1 Take a right on Lower Road (dirt).

0.6 Turn left on Windsor Bush Road, which in 0.1 mile turns into a trail at someone's house. Coast down the grassy doubletrack to an intriguing bridge. Its side supports are a network fabricated from various gauge plumbing pipes, all painted orange. Dismount and you should cross without incident.

0.8 Phelps Brook crosses the trail and can be quite deep. Don't despair, hints of a side trail appear in the mass of branches above the trail to the left.

·Jammin' the Jambs

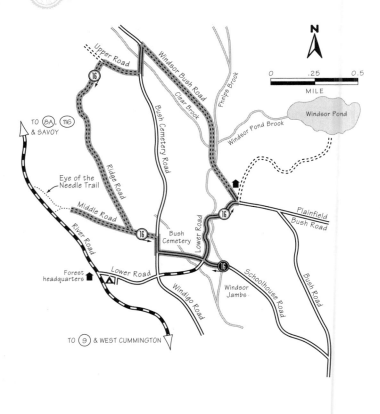

0.9 After the crossing, the trail is smooth and fast-going, with a net gain in elevation for about a mile.

1.8 Take a left onto Bush Cemetery Road, a graded road that suffers wickedly in mud season. On the right, Windsor Bush Road continues as a driveable dirt road.

1.9 About 30 yards after crossing a bridge, turn right onto the trail-like Upper Road.

2.0 Bear left onto Ridge Road. Ridge Road rolls through a lush fir forest, dark, moist, and smelling of earth. The doubletrack trail is without obstacle, carpeted by needles. Moss grows everywhere, and rock hollows look like perfect animal homes.

3.5 Turn right onto Middle Road. You'll climb gently, encountering some hardwoods and a little more light. If you want to cut the ride short, turn left and skip to mile 4.3.

3.9 Middle Road ends at the Needle's Eye Trail, a winding singletrack descent that only experts might enjoy. This shoots you right down to the day use parking lot on River Road. Otherwise, coast back down Middle Road.

4.3 Stay straight on Middle Road as you pass Ridge Road on the left.

4.5 Turn right when you intersect Bush Cemetery Road. A cemetery, enclosed by stone walls and a rusted wrought-iron gate, dates to the 1840s. After a few hundred yards, take your first left, onto Schoolhouse Road. Crane your neck back to see the old steel road sign, originally black letters painted on white, now red with rust.

4.9 Cross Lower Road.

5.0 You're back at the Jambs, all the better from doses of exercise, spectacular scenery, and New England history.

Ashuwillticook Rail-Trail

Location: Lanesborough to Adams and back.

Distance: 21.2 miles out and back with infinite options. You can turn around whenever you like, and roads cross the trail regularly, providing alternative starting points. A popular option is to begin in Cheshire and ride to Adams and back, because this segment is the most wild and wooded.

Time: 1.5 to 3 hours.

Tread: Doubletrack. For now. This trail is slated to become 10 feet wide and paved in an undetermined upcoming year. Funding is slow. Enjoy this while you can!

Aerobic level: Easy.

Technical difficulty: 2. There are occasional patches of course gravel and a few sandy spots.

Hazards: Falling asleep on the bike because all you see, mile after mile, is the trail ahead of you, shrinking into the horizon.

Highlights: No technical obstacles! No hills! No following directions! Views of Mt. Greylock and wildflowers are

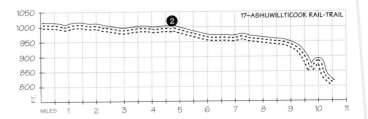

grand, and provide a different aesthetic for those bored of trees: backyard laundry lines, gutted factories, and graffiti-covered railroad bridges.

Land status: Massachusetts Executive Office of Transportation (EOTC).

Maps: USGS Pittsfield East, Cheshire, North Adams.

Access: From the junction of Massachusetts Routes 8 and 9 in Coltsville, head north on Route 8. After 1.6 miles, turn left onto Berkshire Mall Road. The trailhead is 50 feet from the turn, but drive up and park at the Berkshire Mall.

The ride

0.0 From the junction of the railroad tracks and Berkshire Mall Road, head north on the trail.

0.9 Here comes 0.2 mile of gravel hazard. Stay loose, lulled by the sound of Route 8 traffic, and ride through it.

1.5 Pass the first house.

1.7 Cross a paved road (Summer Street).

2.3 Cross under power lines.

2.4 Cross a dirt road (Nobodys Road).

2.8 The Cheshire Reservoir comes into view on your left. In summertime, the trail becomes a corridor of colorful allergens!

3.7 A gravel patch waits here. Cross an anonymous paved road.

3.9 Mt. Greylock looms over the reservoir.

4.3 Keep your eyes open. You may see a grazing donkey on the right.

5.0 Rubble patch.

5.1 Cross Route 8, and ride through more rubble.

5.3 Cross a railroad bridge.

·Ashuwillticook Rail-Trail

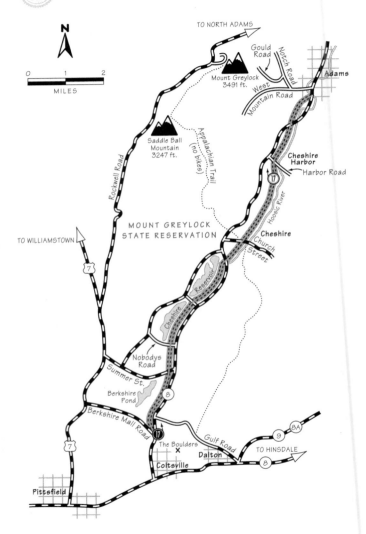

TO NORTH ADAMS

Gould Road

N

Notch Road

0 1 2
MILES

Adams

Mount Greylock
3491 ft.

West
Mountain Road

Saddle Ball
Mountain
3247 ft.

Appalachian Trail
(no bikes)

Cheshire
Harbor

Rockwell Road

17

Harbor Road

Hoosic River

MOUNT GREYLOCK
STATE RESERVATION

TO WILLIAMSTOWN

Cheshire

7

Church
Street

Reservoir

Cheshire

Nobodys
Road

Summer St.

8

Berkshire
Pond

Berkshire Mall Road

9 8A

7

17

Gulf Road

TO HINSDALE

The Boulders
×

Coltsville

Dalton

8

Pittsfield

5.6 Cross a dirt road. The intersection is decorated by an immobile, red Ford pickup.

5.9 Cross a paved road (Church Street). The Hoosic River joins over your right shoulder.

8.0 The first building in a long time, an old power station, appears on the left. Just beyond it stands a red brick pumping station.

8.2 Ride through some gravel, cross a bridge, and cross a dirt road (Harbor Road). You've reached Cheshire Harbor, once a refuge for runaway slaves.

8.4 Take a look at the dam on the left, followed by a large industrial building without windows.

9.3 Cross another patch of rubble.

9.5 Cross under Route 8.

9.6 The trail merges into dirt road. Follow the road and within a tenth of a mile all is back to normal.

10.0 Cross under a road.

10.2 Cross a paved road (Fisk Road). If you're lucky, there'll be a Little League game taking place on your left.

10.6 The trail ends in Adams, beside the Greylock Federal Credit Union. Take a look around town, then turn around and head home.

21.2 You're back at the mall.

October Mountain—
Boulder Trail Loop

Location: Washington.

Distance: 4.9-mile loop.

Time: 0.5 to 1 hour.

Tread: 3.9 miles on doubletrack; 1 mile on dirt road.

Aerobic level: Easy.

Technical difficulty: 3 and 4. In parts, Navin Trail is a bed of rocks with patches of dirt.

Hazards: Sliding through mud on the upper section of Navin Trail.

Highlights: Picking a super line through a rocky splay on the Boulder Trail, evergreens surrounding and a stream babbling at your side.

Land status: October Mountain State Forest (DEM).

Maps: USGS East Lee, Pittsfield East; DEM October Mountain State Forest.

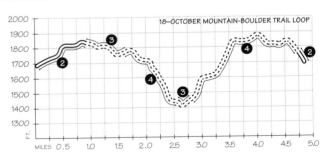

Access: From the intersection of Massachusetts Route 102 and U.S. Route 20 in Lee, take Route 20 west though the center of town. After 1.1 miles, turn right on Center Street at Joe's Diner (made famous by Norman Rockwell). Follow brown State Park signs. From forest headquarters, follow Woodland Road north. After 0.8 mile, turn right onto Roaring Brook Road (dirt). After 0.3 mile, turn right onto Schermerhorn Road (paved), a steep uphill. Drive to where the pavement ends in 0.8 mile and park in the dirt lot on the left side of the road.

The ride

0.0 From the parking area, turn left and begin climbing up Schermerhorn Road, now dirt.

0.1 Boulder Trail leaves from the right.

0.2 Pass a second Boulder Trail entrance on the right.

0.6 A trail leaves from the left.

0.8 Take a right on Spruce Trail.

0.9 Bear right as another Spruce entry joins from the left. Cruise easily on level terrain cushioned by spruce needles.

1.6 Turn right onto Navin Trail. The next half-mile sports rocks and mud.

2.0 A trail that cuts over to the Boulder Trail leaves through a stone wall on the right. Continue straight, downhill on Navin Trail, which hints of streambed.

2.5 With a large circular water tower in view on the left, bear right onto Boulder Trail. The trail is smooth and flat, but not for long. Soon you will be picking your line between basketball-size rocks as you roll through the streamside fir forest.

2.9 The trail levels.

3.9 The descent begins.

·Boulder Trail Loop

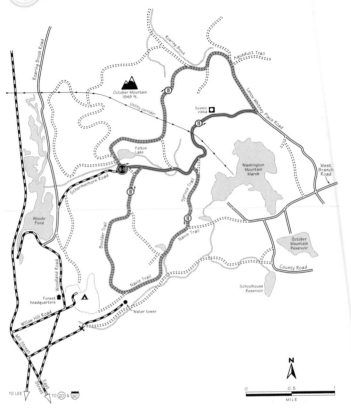

4.5 Bear right when Boulder Trail forks.

4.7 Boulder Trail ends at Schermerhorn Road (dirt). Take a left and coast down the road.

4.9 You're back at the parking lot. This ride can be paired with Ride 19, which also leaves from this parking lot.

October Mountain— Felton Lake Loop

Location: Washington.

Distance: 5.8-mile loop.

Time: 1 to 1.75 hours.

Tread: 3.4 miles on doubletrack; 2.4 miles on dirt road.

Aerobic level: Moderate.

Technical difficulty: 4.

Hazards: Colliding into the lip of the bridge at mile 5.4 because the scenery had you daydreaming.

Highlights: Feeling you've got this whole huge forest to yourself.

Land status: October Mountain State Forest (DEM).

Maps: USGS East Lee, Pittsfield East; DEM October Mountain State Forest.

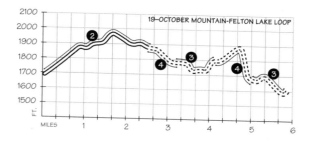

·Felton Lake Loop

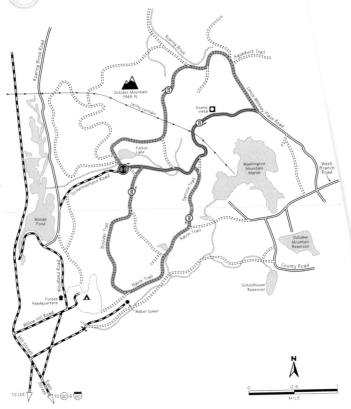

Access: From the intersection of Massachusetts Route 102 and U.S. Route 20 in Lee, take Route 20 (which becomes Main Street). After 1.1 miles, turn right on Center Street at Joe's Diner (made famous by Norman Rockwell). Follow brown State Park signs. From forest headquarters, follow

Woodland Road north. After 0.8 mile, turn right onto Roaring Brook Road (dirt). After 0.3 mile, turn right onto Schermerhorn Road (paved), a steep uphill. Drive to where the pavement ends in 0.8 mile and park in the dirt lot on the left side of the road.

The ride

0.0 From the parking area, turn left and begin climbing up Schermerhorn Road, now dirt.

1.6 On your left is Anderson Vista. Try to find Mt. Greylock.

2.3 Take a left on Lenox–Whitney Place Road (dirt), which descends in both elevation and road quality.

2.9 Aqueduct Trail, wide and roadlike, Ts in on the right. Continue straight.

3.0 A skinny doubletrack trail veers left from the road. Take this rocky and frequently damp trail.

3.4 The trail forks. Go right.

3.5 Cross a wooden bridge.

3.8 Cross another wooden bridge.

3.9 The trail forks just near the bottom of a short downhill. Bear left, up a gradual hill.

4.1 Cross a bridge. Here begins a series of four technical steeps.

4.6 Turn left when the trail Ts into the utility corridor. After about 50 feet, follow the trail as it curves right, off the path of the grassy corridor. This takes you down a rocky downhill through a tunnel of thorns. Sounds masochistic, but remember, a tunnel of thorns, in the appropriate months, is a tunnel of raspberries.

4.7 Take a 90-degree right turn. A stump marks the junction. Continue the rocky descent.

4.9 Rocks become scarcer and cruising speed increases.

5.2 A short steep takes you to a streamside cove of fir trees, on soft pine-needle-coated terrain. Pretty heavenly. If the bugs aren't out, sprawl out for a rest.

5.4 Pick a good line over that bridge!

5.5 Take a 90-degree left down a singletrack trail. Just after the turn, a chimney, the only remnant of a house, stands high. Just down the hill, a trail merges in on the right.

5.6 Arrive at a skewed four-way intersection. Take the left, down to Felton Lake. Take a moment to enjoy its endearing lily pads. Leaving the pond, bear left up the rubble road.

5.8 Return to the parking lot. Check out Ride 18, which also leaves from this parking lot, if you're up for more.

October Mountain— Ashley Lake Loop

Location: Washington.

Distance: 9-mile loop.

Time: 1.25 to 2.5 hours.

Tread: 5.7 miles on doubletrack; 0.9 mile on dirt road; 2.4 miles on paved road.

Aerobic level: Moderate.

Technical difficulty: 3.

Hazards: Getting caught in a fierce May snow squall.

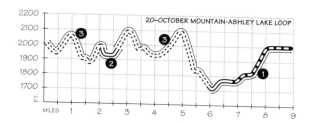

Highlights: Cruising a loop high in spectacular views and low in muscular anguish through the deep 16,000-acre woods of the largest state forest in Massachusetts; resting on a boulder beside deep blue Ashley Lake; watching a reservoir-fed fountain jet water 15 feet in the air.

Land status: October Mountain State Forest (DEM).

Maps: USGS Pittsfield East; DEM October Mountain State Forest.

Access: From North Street (U.S. Route 7) in Pittsfield, take Park Plaza (the road which loops around Park Square) to East Street. Half a mile from North Street, turn right onto Elm Street. After 2 miles, bear left onto Williams Street. Go 1 mile on Williams Street. At Burgner Farm, bear right onto Washington Mountain Road. Stay to the right on Washington Mountain Road as Kirchner Road veers left after 0.1 mile. Follow Washington Mountain Road, which becomes Pittsfield Road, 4.7 miles to the Appalachian Trail (AT) trailhead.

The ride

0.0 Follow the Appalachian Trail toward Georgia west and south. (In this part the trail looks like a dirt road.) When the AT turns left as a distinct hiking trail, continue straight. Ashley Lake on the right

• Ashley Lake Loop

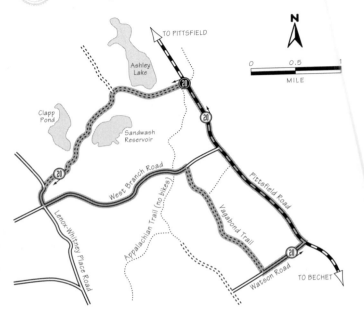

makes a fine spot for a picnic, with boulders to sit on and a view of the lake's dark blue waters.

0.9 Follow the main trail past two unmarked right-hand turnoffs. Continue up the gradual, wide slope to Sandwash Reservoir, which supplies Pittsfield with drinking water. The trail climbs another 20 yards, then curves left and descends gradually. Keep your eyes peeled to the left, where a reservoir-fed fountain jets water 15 feet in the air. A gradual downhill rolls you out to Lenox–Whitney Place Road.

2.3 Take a left on Whitney Place Road, a dirt road.

2.6 At a four-way intersection of dirt roads, take a left up West Branch Road. The road begins with a rock-strewn incline. Make it up and the descent is all yours.

4.4 About 100 yards past where the AT crosses the trail, turn right on the Vagabond Trail, marked by a brown and white sign. The trail climbs through the woods for 0.3 mile, then turns into a smooth, long gradual descent. Take advantage of this rare luxury—pedal occasionally, admire trees as you pass by, and take a swig from your water bottle.

6.0 The Vagabond Trail Ts into Watson Road. Turn left.

6.6 Take a left onto Pittsfield Road, a paved road. Gaining elevation is so easy on pavement!

9.0 Return to parking spot.

South County

If you're looking for the place with the most challenging and unrepetitive riding in the area, Beartown State Forest, where mud season lasts until September and no month is safe from snow squalls, can't be beat. Beartown is, in the words of the West Virginia license plate, wild and wonderful. The park covers four towns, but you won't find yourself popping out across from a local diner with a handpainted sign for hot apple pie. Roving 23 miles of trails, plus a network of surrounding dirt roads, you're more likely to come across a blue heron, logging enterprise, or deer carcass. Ride 21, a road ride, offers access to the forest when bugs and mud would otherwise keep you away. Otherwise, gather up a crowd of friends on a sunny morning and head to Ride 22.

Mt. Washington packs the odd combination of quaint cozy Southern Berkshires nature with harshness reminiscent of the Rockies. Babbling brooks invite swimming, oak leaves seem to capture gold light independent of season, and clover covers fields edged by cow-containing stone walls. Twenty minutes of biking later, you'll find yourself fending off hypothermia on a wind-raked mountaintop, wondering at the landscape below. Around you, rugged scrub oak and pitch pine grow from granite, and a deserted fire tower alludes to times past.

In case you tire of speeds under 10 miles an hour, three road loops, Rides 23, 24, and 27, swing you through some of the most spectacular scenery in the Southern Berkshires.

Beartown— Mt. Wilcox Road Loop

Location: Great Barrington.

Distance: 14.9-mile loop.

Time: 1.5 to 2 hours.

Tread: 8.4 miles on dirt road; 6.5 miles on paved road.

Aerobic level: Strenuous. Roller-coaster terrain plum sucks the wind from anyone.

Technical difficulty: 1 to 2, with sections of 3 (which coincide with the steepest uphill sections).

Hazards: Speeding confidently down a paved road and happening upon a huge bulging anthill of buckling pavement.

Highlights: Experiencing spring in Beartown without fixing your bike with pontoons.

Land status: Beartown State Forest (DEM).

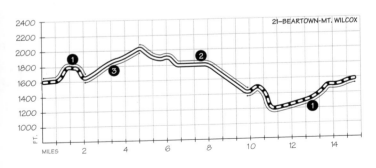

Maps: USGS Great Barrington, Otis; DEM Beartown State Forest.

Access: From the intersection of U.S. Highway 7 and Massachusetts Route 23 in Great Barrington, drive east on Route 23 4.4 miles. Turn left onto Brett Road (paved), then after 0.4 mile, turn left onto Blue Hill Road. Forest headquarters, which has maps for the taking, is located at this intersection. After 1.4 miles, turn right on Benedict Pond Road (paved). Follow this 0.5 mile to the Benedict Pond Visitors Center whose picnic tables, restrooms, and pay phone complement a peaceful swimming lake. Park here. During the summer, parking will cost $2.00.

The ride

0.0 From the Benedict Pond Visitors Center, head north on Beartown Road. The pavement allows for a fast-rolling warm-up, but keep your eye out for frost heaves, divots, and bulges in the road.

0.2 A campground is on the right.

2.0 Pay homage to the tombstonelike bald tree trunks in the beaver pond on your right.

2.1 Take the hairpin right onto Mt. Wilcox Road, a rugged dirt road. A tenth of a mile steep section at mile 2.5 introduces you to the quickly changing array of grades that characterize the climb up Mt. Wilcox.

3.1 A power line descends on the right.

3.5 In August, it would be rude not to stop for the receiving line of blackberries.

4.3 The road forks; turn left. This dirt road spur climbs to the top of Mt. Wilcox.

4.4 At the summit, sprawl on the grassy section at the base of the fire tower. Views of Berkshire farmland stretch to the east. Follow the same spur you took up

· Mt. Wilcox Road Loop

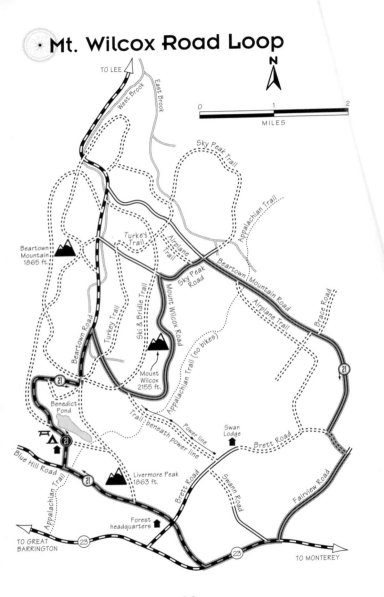

N

TO LEE

West Brook

East Brook

Sky Peak Trail

Appalachian Trail

0   1   2
MILES

Turkey Trail

Airplane Trail

Beartown Mountain Road

Beartown Mountain 1865 ft.

Sky Peak Road

Brace Road

Turkey Trail

Ski & Bridle Trail

Mount Wilcox Road

Airplane Trail

Beartown Road

Mount Wilcox 2155 ft.

Appalachian Trail (no bikes)

21

21

Benedict Pond

Appalachian Trail

Trail beneath power line

Power line

Swan Lodge

Brett Road

Blue Hill Road

21

Livermore Peak 1863 ft.

Brett Road

Swann Road

Fairview Road

Forest headquarters

TO GREAT BARRINGTON

23

23

TO MONTEREY

100

back down to Mt. Wilcox Road. Turn left. Carry your speed on the descent because the road has no tricky turns and soon levels out.

5.6 Mt. Wilcox Road Ts into Sky Peak Road; turn right.

6.3 Sky Peak Road Ts into Beartown Mountain Road; turn right.

7.4 In the midst of this wild, a house!

9.7 The road turns to pavement. Within 100 feet, turn right onto Fairview Road (paved). Hopefully you have some affection left for short, steep uphills.

10.3 The road turns from pavement to dirt.

11.1 Fairview Ts into Massachusetts Route 23; turn right.

12.1 Turn right onto Blue Hill Road (paved).

12.8 Cross Brett Road, passing Forest headquarters on your left. Keep your eyes open for baying animals as you ride beside pastures.

14.4 Turn right on Benedict Pond Road (paved).

14.9 Return to Benedict Pond Visitors Center.

Beartown Trails Epic

Location: Lee.

Distance: 17-mile loop, with several opportunities to shorten.

Time: 2.5 to 4 hours.

Tread: 13 miles of doubletrack; 2.8 miles of paved road; 1.2 miles of dirt road.

Aerobic level: Strenuous.

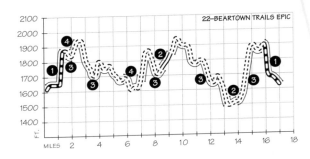

Technical difficulty: 3 and 4.

Hazards: Mud—call ahead for trail conditions.

Highlights: Riding deep in the woods, imagining yourself as Thoreau.

Land status: Beartown State Forest (DEM).

Maps: USGS Great Barrington, Otis; DEM Beartown State Forest.

Access: From the intersection of U.S. Route 7 and Massachusetts Route 102 in Stockbridge, take Route 102. After 1.6 miles, turn right, across the Housatonic River, into what looks like the parking lot for a Mead Paper factory (the side of the red brick factory reads "Hurlbut Papers Willow Mill" in white paint), but is actually Willow Street. Willow Street merges into Beartown Mountain Road, the forest's main drag; from Mead it's 3.8 miles to the CCC Camp on the right-hand side of the road. Park here.

The ride

- **0.0** From the southern end of the CCC Camp parking lot, start your odometer and head south.
- **1.4** Turn left up a doubletrack labeled SKI AND BRIDLE TRAIL. This little steep will make you appreciate your on-road warm-up.

1.5 Take a left on Turkey Trail, picking a line amid rocks sticking up like the heads of helmeted motorcyclists.

1.8 Take a left on Wilcox Road (dirt), and an immediate right on Turkey Trail.

1.9 Loose rocks make things tricky for 0.2 mile.

2.1 Let the cruising begin. Without a rock to be found, bright orange summertime salamanders may be your only obstacles.

2.9 Maneuver a short technical portion, then cross river.

3.4 Ibid.

3.6 Cross Sky Peak Road (dirt).

3.8 Stay quick up a tricky uphill section. Rocks abound, and the rubber water bars aren't as flexible as you'd like.

4.4 Cross the Ski and Bridle Trail. Jitter up a short hill (the last one for this segment!), then take in the bliss of the ensuing soft, windy descent.

4.9 Airplane Trail Ts in on the right.

5.2 The trail ends on Beartown Mountain Road (dirt). Take a left, and after 50 feet, turn right onto Sky Peak Trail, which at this section is as wide as a dirt road. (To lop off 2.6 miles of doubletrack from the route, turn right on the road and ride for 0.7 mile to the four-way intersection described at mile 8.5 of this ride.)

5.4 A trail turns off to the left. Stay right, crossing the bridge alongside the beaver pond. The trail begins smooth and fast.

5.9 A rocky uphill greets you.

6.3 The next half-mile is rockier than the norm, and often damp and buggy.

6.9 Cross a stream, then climb a steep, short hill.

8.1 The trail widens significantly, becoming roadlike as you head gradually up.

⋅ Beartown Trails Epic

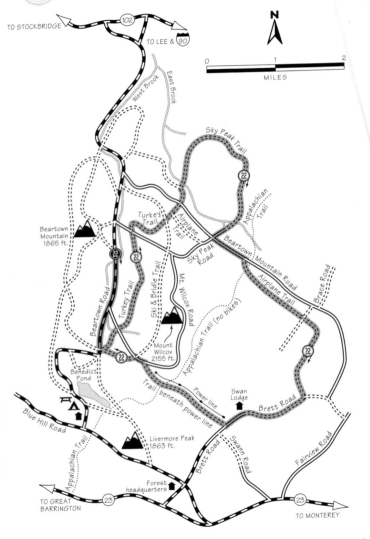

TO STOCKBRIDGE

102

TO LEE & 90

N

0 1 2
MILES

West Brook

East Brook

Sky Peak Trail

22

Appalachian Trail

Turkey Trail

Airplane Trail

Beartown Mountain 1865 ft.

Beartown Mountain Road

Airplane Trail

Brace Road

Sky Peak Road

22

22

Turkey Trail

Ski & Bridle Trail

Mt. Wilcox Road

Beartown Road

Appalachian Trail (no bikes)

22

Mount Wilcox 2155 ft.

22

Benedict Pond

Power line

Swan Lodge

Brett Road

Trail beneath power line

Blue Hill Road

Livermore Peak 1863 ft.

Brett Road

Swann Road

Fairview Road

Appalachian Trail

Forest headquarters

TO GREAT BARRINGTON

23

TO MONTEREY

23

8.5 Reach a four-way intersection. Turn left.

9.0 Take a right on Airplane Trail, a rooted dirt double-track. A sign marks the trail.

9.2 Cross the Appalachian Trail.

9.3 Cross a stream.

10.2 Cross another stream, on a rather high bridge.

10.5 Cross a grass-up-the-middle doubletrack (McCarthy Road). Airplane Trail gets a bit skinnier briefly.

10.8 Coast through a sea of aromatic ferns. But ferns signal moisture, and sure enough here comes the gully of mud.

12.1 Turn right on Brett Road, a wide trail. You'll cross a stream, then head up a hill sprinkled with loose rubble.

12.7 Pass through a pair of stone pillars, the entrance to the Swann Estate and starting gate for a fast, straight descent.

13.1 Swann Lodge, a red farmhouse, stands on the right. The Lodge, willed to the state by the Swann family, serves a number of functions, among them hosting Elderhostel events and introducing kids from the city to the great outdoors. Past the lodge, Brett Road becomes a real road, suitable for Cadillacs.

13.4 Take a right onto the grassy doubletrack trail that runs directly under the power line, descending easily.

13.5 Suddenly the trail becomes wet. A quick investigative glance and you will notice that the trail runs below the water level of the tree-cemetery beaver pond on your right. Take a good look around and you may see some exciting birds in the pond. Now it's time for the climb!

14.3 Downhill, an unexpected respite from the uphill.

14.5 Wouldn't you know it, just as you're fully anaerobic, the trail turns technical.

14.8 The trail turns grassy.

14.9 Turn left on Mt. Wilcox Road (dirt). The allure of a fast dirt road descent after all that climbing is high, but check your speed and watch for the next turn—it's an easy one to miss. (If you want to hasten your return to the car, stay on the road, then turn right when you intersect with Beartown Mountain Road.)

15.3 Turn left on Ski and Bridle Trail.

15.4 Turkey Trail merges in from the right.

15.6 Pop out on Beartown Mountain Road. Turn right and cruise downhill to your car.

17.0 You're back at the CCC Camp parking lot.

23

Sheffield Flats Road Loop

Location: Sheffield.

Distance: 16.7-mile loop.

Time: 1.5 to 2.5 hours.

Tread: 10.5 miles on dirt road; 6.2 miles on paved road.

Aerobic level: Easy.

Technical difficulty: 2.

Hazards: Being so struck by gorgeous farmland that you give it all up—the job, the car, the Web—to go subsistence.

Highlights: Cruising past a field of lowing Holsteins.

Land status: Town roads.

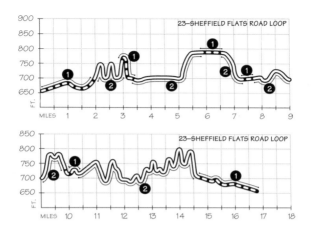

Maps: USGS Great Barrington, Ashley Falls.

Access: The ride starts in the center of Sheffield, at the Sheffield Post Office on U.S. Route 7. Candees Restaurant, the Sheffield Market, and Berkshire Bank are also on-site.

The ride

0.0 Head north on Route 7. The next 1.3-mile stretch is the necessary evil of this otherwise lovely ride.

1.3 Turn left on Egremont Road (paved), which goes diagonally northwest, up a slight hill and across a set of train tracks.

2.1 Turn right on West Road (dirt).

3.0 West Road turns to pavement.

3.1 Turn left on Lime Kiln Road (paved).

3.4 Bear left onto the now-dirt Lime Kiln Road as Rebellion Road (paved) veers right.

3.7 Cross Sheffield-Egremont Road. A huge flat expanse of farmland extends before you, with Mt. Everett and its neighboring hills as a backdrop.

Sheffield Flats Road Loop

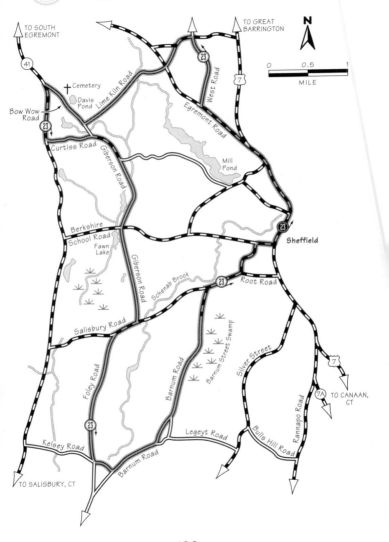

TO SOUTH EGREMONT

TO GREAT BARRINGTON

N

41

Cemetery

Davis Pond

Lime Kiln Road

Bow Wow Road

23

Curtiss Road

Giberson Road

West Road

7

Egremont Road

Mill Pond

0   0.5   1
MILE

23

Sheffield

Berkshire School Road

Fawn Lake

Giberson Road

Schenab Brook

23

Root Road

Salisbury Road

Barnum Street Swamp

Silver Street

Foley Road

Barnum Road

7

7A   TO CANAAN, CT

Rannapo Road

23

Legeyt Road

Bulls Hill Road

Kelsey Road

Barnum Road

TO SALISBURY, CT

5.0 When you T into Bow Wow Road (dirt), turn right. Corn hugs the road on the right; on the left trees are draped top-to-bottom in vines.

5.2 A white wooden fence encloses an old cemetery, where tall white pines shade weathered gravestones dated as early as 1758.

5.8 Turn left on Massachusetts Route 41 (paved).

6.6 Turn left onto Curtiss Road (dirt).

7.2 Turn right on Bow Wow Road (paved).

7.6 Turn right on Giberson Road (dirt).

7.9 As you pass through a swamp, the road gets damp.

8.1 An uphill. Calling this a hill indicates how flat this ride is!

7.4 More swamp all around you.

8.7 Cross Berkshire School Road, heading into a dark tunnel of trees on a road often overgrown with grass.

9.3 Hearty old sugar maples line the narrow road. The forest begins to change, and soon you are riding through damp greenery.

10.1 Turn right on Salisbury Road (paved).

10.3 Turn left on Foley Road (paved).

10.4 The road turns to dirt. It's much wider than Giberson and has new houses and lawns alongside it.

11.3 A giant weeping willow in all its grandeur stands on the left.

12.0 At a four-way intersection, turn left on Kelsey Road (dirt).

12.3 Just past a snazzy new house built onto an old red barn, turn left on Barnum Road (dirt).

12.4 Bear left as Veeley Road goes right. Watch for cows here.

13.0 Bear left at the fork.

13.5 A dirt road joins from the right.

14.1 Watch for the flower gardens on the left!

14.5 The road turns to pavement. On the right is a Massachusetts Audubon Society wildlife sanctuary; on the left the Sheffield town dump.

15.2 Turn right on Salisbury Road (paved).

15.3 Another cemetery on the left, this one hidden by a huge hedge.

16.1 On the right, a tree grows vigorously out of a wooden shed.

16.2 Turn right on Berkshire School Road (paved).

16.5 Turn left on Route 7.

16.7 The parking lot is on your left.

Thousand Acre Swamp Road Loop

Location: Southfield.

Distance: 12.6-mile loop.

Time: 1 to 2 hours.

Tread: 9.2 miles on dirt road; 3.4 miles on paved road.

Aerobic level: Moderate.

Technical difficulty: 2.

Hazards: Mud season can wreak havoc (and let slip the dogs of war) on these roads.

Highlights: Standing in wonder watching great blue herons in Thousand Acre Swamp.

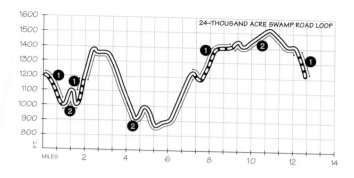

24–THOUSAND ACRE SWAMP ROAD LOOP

Land status: Town roads.

Maps: USGS Tolland Center.

Access: From the junction of U.S. Route 7 and Massachusetts Route 23 in Great Barrington, head east on Route 23. After 3.5 miles, turn right on Massachusetts Route 57. Go 5.8 miles, then turn right on New Marlborough–Southfield Road. After another 1.7 miles, park on the side of the road in front of the Southfield Store.

The ride

0.0 Ride south on Norfolk Road, as New Marlborough-Southfield Road is called south of Southfield.

0.4 Turn right on Canaan-Southfield Road (paved).

0.7 Bear right.

1.0 Veer right onto Keyes Hill Road (dirt). A farm with magnificent stone walls awaits you at the top.

1.5 At the five-way intersection, cross the intersection onto Rhodes and Bailey Road.

1.9 Cagney Road joins from the right; turn left and continue on Rhodes and Bailey Road (dirt).

4.5 When the road turns into Cross Road (dirt), turn left.

5.0 Turn left on an unmarked dirt road.

Thousand Acre Swamp Road Loop

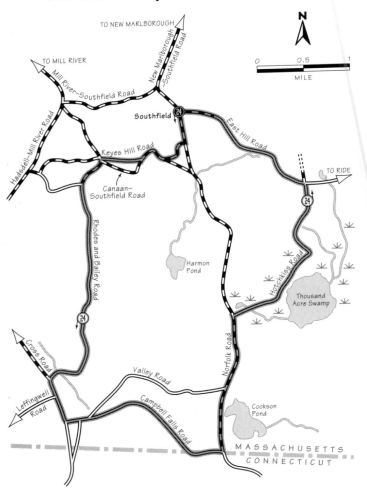

TO NEW MARLBOROUGH

TO MILL RIVER

Mill River–Southfield Road

New Marlborough–Southfield Road

Southfield

24

East Hill Road

Hadsdell–Mill River Road

Keyes Hill Road

Canaan–Southfield Road

Rhodes and Bailey Road

24

TO RIDE

24

Hotchkiss Road

Harmon Pond

Thousand Acre Swamp

Cross Road

Valley Road

Norfolk Road

Campbell Falls Road

Cookson Pond

Leffingwell Road

MASSACHUSETTS
CONNECTICUT

N

0   0.5   1
MILE

5.2	A dirt road joins from the right.
5.3	At the Y, bear right on Campbell Falls Road.
6.6	Cross an old bridge with stone sides.
6.8	A pullout on the right side of the road gives access to hiking trails to Campbell Falls. The view of the falls from the bottom of the ravine is well worth the short hike.
7.1	Turn left on Norfolk Road (paved).
8.7	Turn right on Hotchkiss Road (paved, then turns immediately to dirt) and begin going uphill.
9.1	Cruise down a fast descent.
9.3	A 0.05-mile side road on the right goes to the Thousand Acre Swamp, part of Cookson State Forest.
10.8	Turn left on East Hill Road (dirt).
12.2	The road turns to pavement.
12.6	You're back at the Southfield Store and the car.

Mt. Washington— Ashley Hill Jaunt

Location: Mount Washington. (Ever heard of this place? In the southwestern corner of the state, it's the smallest town in Berkshire County, with 120 year-round residents.)

Distance: 8.8-mile lollipop.

Time: 1 to 2 hours.

Tread: Doubletrack.

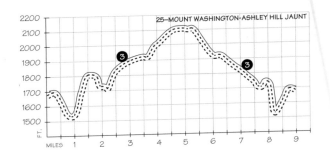

Aerobic level: Easy.

Technical difficulty: 3.

Hazards: Losing track of time because the scenery is so stellar.

Highlights: Starting the ride through a field of clover edged by bovine-proof stone walls; cruising beside a scenic brook sheltered by healthy trees; and stopping frequently at swimming holes, each one better than the last.

Land status: Mt. Washington State Forest (DEM).

Maps: USGS Ashley Falls; DEM Mt. Washington State Forest Trail Map.

Access: From the intersection of Massachusetts Route 23 and U.S. Route 7 in Great Barrington, take Route 23 west. After 4.2 miles, turn left onto Massachusetts Route 41, then right onto Mt. Washington Road after 0.2 mile. Follow the pavement, and the signs, 9.8 miles to Mt. Washington State Forest.

The ride

0.0 From the western edge of forest headquarters, ride the doubletrack trail through the break in the stone wall and into a wide-open field.

· Ashley Hill Jaunt

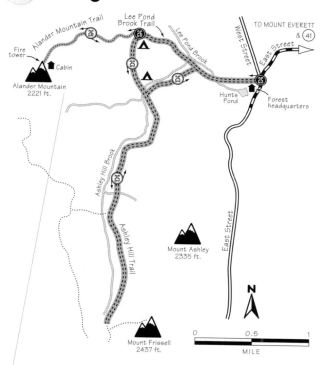

0.7 Bear right at the intersection, following signs to Alander Mountain.

1.4 The trail to Alander Mountain goes right. See Ride 26 if you're up for the challenge. Otherwise, turn left.

2.1 Cross Ashley Hill Brook.

2.2 Take a right on Ashley Hill Trail, which follows Ashley Hill Brook. Mountain biking at its mellowist and most scenic! The incline is so slight you won't even notice you're going uphill.

3.7 A hiking trail turns off on the right. Stay left.

4.9 There had to be one flaw, didn't there? Yup, this ride's an out-and-back. Turn around. The hiking trail on your left may look tempting, but unless you enjoy your bike as an external frame pack over several miles of extremely tricky terrain, pass it up.

7.6 Take a right.

8.1 Bear right.

8.8 You're home, and a better person for it. If you're in the mood for some more scenery, hop in the car and head to Bash Bish Falls, a noisy and dramatic waterfall and popular summer cooling-off spot. To get to Bash Bish Falls, leave the way you came. After 1.7 miles, turn left, following the sign. From here, it's 3.3 miles to a parking lot on the left from where trails (0.2 mile) descend to the falls.

Mt. Washington— Alander Mountain

Location: Mount Washington.

Distance: 2.4-mile out-and-back.

Time: 1 hour.

Tread: Singletrack.

Aerobic level: Strenuous.

Technical difficulty: 4 to 5. This is technical New England riding at its best.

Hazards: Careening off rocks and roots, getting chilled on a wind-raked summit.

Highlights: Climbing to a bald-topped summit where rugged scrub oak and pitch pine cling to granite and a deserted fire tower alludes to times past.

Land status: Mt. Washington State Forest (DEM).

Maps: USGS Ashley Falls; DEM Mt. Washington State Forest.

Access: This ride begins at mile 1.4 of Ride 25.

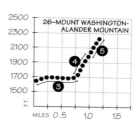

The ride

0.0 From the intersection of Lee Pond Brook Trail and Alander Mountain Trail (mile 1.4 of ride 25), take Alander Mountain Trail. Enjoy the lush forest while the biking doesn't require your full attention. It will soon.

0.7 The climb becomes steep and narrow. We're talking granny gear all the way. Try to keep your front wheel earth-borne as you bounce off jutting rocks.

1.1 Near the top sits a tiny ramshackle cabin, a quirky home for the weary backpacker. Vintage hot chocolate mix and rusted cans of sardines may save you in a pinch, and a hikers' log makes for interesting reading. On the door a note signed "the Woods" reminds people to carry out their garbage, and they listen—the

· Alander Mountain

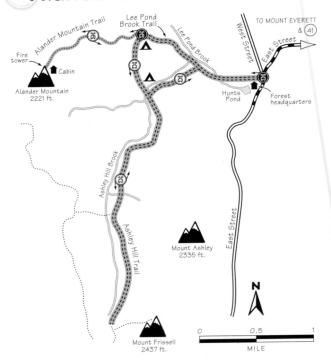

beauty of the land in this state forest is amazingly well preserved.

1.2 Climb your way to the summit and peer out over New York farmland to the Catskills. On a good day, you can see the Albany skyline. When you've had your fill, turn around for the exciting route down.

2.4 Either leave the way you came, or resume Ride 25 at mile 1.4.

27

Sandisfield Road Loop

Location: Sandisfield.

Distance: 15.8-mile loop.

Time: 1.25 to 2.25 hours.

Tread: 13.1 miles on dirt road; 2.7 miles on paved road.

Aerobic level: Easy.

Technical difficulty: 2.

Hazards: Logging trucks resurfacing the road for you.

Highlights: Maxing out your senses as you hammer up Silverbrook Road, lungs working, legs dripping, eyes wandering through the uninterrupted forest, and breathing in the smell of trees and earth.

Land status: Sandisfield State Forest (DEM) and town roads.

Maps: USGS Tolland Center.

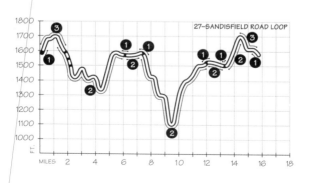

Access: From the junction of U.S. Route 7 and Massachusetts Route 23 in Great Barrington, head east on Route 23. After 3.5 miles, turn right on Massachusetts Route 57. Follow Route 57 another 8.8 miles to a paved road with brown sign that reads YORK LAKE SANDISFIELD STATE FOREST. Turn left here, heading over a one-lane bridge on the edge of the lake, then parking in the lot after 0.3 mile.

The ride

0.0 Continue riding north and east on the road you entered on.

0.3 Turn right on York Lake Road, which is unmarked and will likely have a strip of grass running up its middle. Let your imagination wander to racing with the greats in the Paris-Roubaix.

1.0 Turn right on Sage Road (dirt), another road that doesn't see much traffic.

1.3 Road quality improves as houses appear.

1.7 Turn left on South Sandisfield–New Marlborough Road (paved).

2.4 Turn right on Norfolk Road (dirt).

4.5 Cross South Sandisfield–New Marlborough Road onto Rood Hill Road. Begin the long climb to the road's single house.

6.0 Turn right on South Sandisfield Road (paved).

6.4 Turn right on Gremier Road (dirt).

7.3 Turn right on Sandisfield–New Hartford Road (paved).

7.7 Turn left on Fox Road (dirt), disregarding the ROAD CLOSED DUE TO MUD sign.

9.3 Pass through the four-way junction of dirt roads, with Viets Road on your left and Elk Road on the right. An elk wouldn't be shocking at this rustic intersection.

· Sandisfield Road Loop

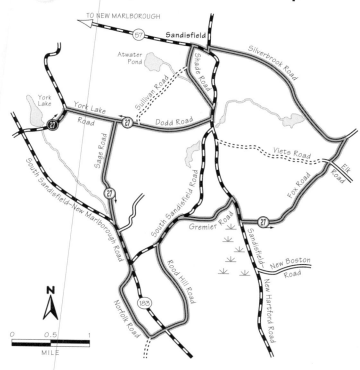

9.7 Turn left on Silverbrook Road (dirt).

12.1 Turn left on New Marlborough–Sandisfield Road (Route 57).

12.4 Turn left on Shade Road (dirt) and ride over the spots of light that make it through the dense over-story.

12.7 At the fork, bear left on Shade Road (don't turn onto Sullivan Road).

13.4 Turn right on Sandisfield–New Hartford Road (paved).

13.5 Turn right on Dodd Road (dirt).

14.3 Dodd Road becomes rough, with grass up the middle.

14.8 Go straight, onto York Lake Road when Sage Road joins on the left.

15.5 Turn left when York Lake Road Ts into the forest road.

15.8 Return to car. York Lake is waiting for you.

Appendix 1

Resources

Massachusetts DEM Regional Headquarters
The source for state forest maps.

P.O. Box 1433
Pittsfield, MA 01202
(413) 442–8928

www.magnet.state.ma.us/dem/forparks.htm

DEM is located at 740 South Street in Pittsfield, off of Massachusetts Route 7 about 0.2 mile north of Dan Fox Drive.

New York Department of Environmental Conservation (DEC)
Owns and manages the land in New York that the Taconic Crest Trail travels over.

50 Wolf Road
Albany, NY 12233
(518) 457–2475

www.dec.state.ny.us

Taconic Hiking Club
Maintains Taconic Crest Trail.

c/o Wolfe
45 Kakely Street
Albany, NY 12208
(518) 482–0424

Williamstown Rural Lands Foundation
Works to conserve Williamstown area land.

P.O. Box 221
Williamstown, MA 01267
(413) 458–2494

Mt. Greylock State Reservation
P.O. Box 138
Lanesborough, MA 01237
(413) 499–4263

Savoy Mountain State Forest
260 Central Shaft Road
Florida, MA 01247
(413) 663–8469

Kennedy Park
Kennedy Park Committee c/o Town Hall
Walker Street
Lenox, MA 01240

Berkshire Natural Resources Council
Coordinates conservation of Yokun Ridge.

20 Bank Row
Pittsfield, MA 01201
(413) 499–0596

Pittsfield State Forest
Cascade Street
Pittsfield, MA 01201
(413) 442–8992

Crane & Company
Owns and maintains the Boulders.

30 South Street
Dalton, MA 01226

Windsor State Forest
River Road
Windsor, MA 01270
(413) 684–0948

October Mountain State Forest
317 Woodland Road
Lee, MA 01238
(413) 243–1778

Beartown State Forest
P.O. Box 97
Monteray, MA 01245
(413) 528–0904

Mt. Washington State Forest
East Street
Mt. Washington, MA 01258
(413) 528–0330

Massachusetts Office of Travel and Tourism
Provides general tourism info, fall foliage reports.

(800) 227–6277
web.massvacation.com

Massachusetts State Forest and Parks Campground Reservation Line
(877) 422–6762

New England Weather Associates
Berkshire County Weather
(413) 499–2627
www.newenglandweather.com

Weather Channel
www.weather.com

Massachusetts Department of Fish and Wildlife (Western District Office)
For information on hunting seasons.

(413) 447–9789
www.state.ma.us/dfwele/dfw

New York Division of Fish and Wildlife (License Sales Bureau)
For information on hunting seasons.
(518) 457–3521
www.dec.state.ny.us/website/dfwmr/worhunt.html

Appendix 2

Getting Involved with the Bike Community

Group Rides
Riding with a group is a great way to learn new routes, push the envelope technically by following a rider slightly better than you, and meet some of the most fun-loving and interesting folks in the county! Group rides of varying levels are everywhere in the Berkshires. Many rides are based out of bike shops. Try the Arcadian Shop and Mean Wheels, both in Lenox, and The Mountain Goat in Williamstown for well-attended and welcoming rides. The local cycling club and racing team, the Berkshire Cycling Association/TOSK Chiropractic, serves as a clearinghouse for ride information.

Berkshire Cycling Association
24 Alba Avenue
Pittsfield, MA 01201-4411
www.berkshirecycling.org

Races
You really can find it all here in the Berkshires! Berkshire Cycling Association runs a racing series at Holiday Farm in Dalton that runs Wednesday nights, May through September. July brings The Arcadian to the Berkshires, a race which as a part of the Pedros New England series draws many of the region's top riders. Come August, it's time for the Rock 'N Rut at Windsor Lake in North Adams.

Trail Maintenance
New England Mountain Bike Association's Berkshire chapter makes its presence known, sponsoring trail work days throughout the summer.

New England Mountain Bike Association (NEMBA)
Box 380557
Cambridge, MA 02238
(800) 576–3622

www.nemba.org

Index of Rides

Jack Rabbit Technical Tests
1   Berlin Mountain Loop
10 Lenox Fire Tower Spur
19 October Mountain—Felton Lake Loop
22 Beartown Trails Epic
26 Mt. Washington—Alander Mountain

Bug-Free Road Loops
11 Dean Hill Road Loop
15 Rolling through the Hilltowns
21 Beartown—Mt. Wilcox Road Loop
23 Sheffield Flats Road Loop
24 Thousand Acre Swamp Road Loop
27 Sandisfield Road Loop

Beginner-Friendly Rides
4   Savoy—Bog Pond Loop
6   Cruising in Kennedy
14 The Boulders—Better than Boulder
16 Windsor—Jammin' the Jambs
17 Ashuwillticook Rail-Trail
25 Mt. Washington—Ashley Hill Jaunt

"And I Forgot the Camera" Scenic All-stars
1   Berlin Mountain Loop
16 Windsor—Jammin' the Jambs
23 Sheffield Flats Road Loop
25 Mt. Washington—Ashley Hill Jaunt
26 Mt. Washington—Alander Mountain

"Wish I Were a Yak" Tough Climbs
1   Berlin Mountain Loop
2   Mt. Greylock—Old Adams Road Loop
3   Mt. Greylock—Bellows Pipe Loop
10 Lenox Fire Tower Spur
13 Pittsfield State Forest Zigzag
26 Mt. Washington—Alander Mountain
27 Sandisfield Road Loop

Try-Not-to-Scream Exciting Downhill Rides
1   Berlin Mountain Loop
2   Mt. Greylock—Old Adams Road Loop
5   Savoy—Downhill-Lover's Delight
8   Yokun Ridge Loop
10 Lenox Fire Tower Spur
13 Pittsfield State Forest Zigzag
26 Mt. Washington—Alander Mountain

Glossary

AT: Short for Appalachian Trail, a hiking-only trail that runs from Georgia to Maine.

Bunny hop: Leaping up, while riding, and lifting both wheels off the ground to jump over an obstacle (or for sheer joy).

Clipless: A type of pedal with a binding that accepts a special cleat on the soles of bike shoes. The cleat clicks in for more control and efficient pedaling and out for safe landings (in theory).

DEM: Short for Massachusetts Department of Environmental Management, the agency that manages state forests and parks.

Doubletrack: A trail, jeep road, ORV route, or other track with either two distinct ribbons of tread, or wide enough to fit two bikes.

Endo: Lifting the rear wheel off the ground and riding (or abruptly not riding) on the front wheel only. Also known, at various degrees of control and finality, as a nose wheelie, "going over the handlebars," and a face plant.

Granny gear: The lowest (easiest) gear, a combination of the smallest of the three chain rings on the bottom bracket spindle (where the pedals and crank arms attach to the bike's frame) and the largest cog in the rear cluster. Shift down to your granny gear for serious climbing.

Hammer: To ride hard; derived from how it feels afterward: "I'm hammered."

Line: The route (or trajectory) between or over obstacles or through turns. Tread or trail refers to the ground you're riding on; the line is the path you choose within the tread (and exists mostly in the eye of the beholder).

Off-the-seat: Moving your butt behind the bike seat and over the rear tire; used for control on extremely steep descents. This position increases braking power, helps prevent endos, and reduces skidding.

ORV: Off-road vehicle; in this book ORV refers to motorbikes and three- and four-wheelers designed for off-road use.

Rigid fork: A front fork without suspension—very retro and sometimes painful.

Singletrack: A trail with a single, bike-width ribbon of tread.

Spin: To pedal at a high number of revolutions per minute. This is good for your heart and your knees.

Spur: A side road or trail that splits off from the main route.

Suspension: A bike with front suspension has a shock-absorbing fork, stem, or head tube. Rear suspension absorbs shock between the rear wheel and frame. A bike with both is said to be fully suspended.

Switchbacks: When a trail goes up a steep slope, it zigzags or switch-backs to ease the gradient of the climb.

TCT: Short for Taconic Crest Trail.

Track stand: Balancing on a bike in one place, without rolling forward appreciably. Cock the front wheel to one side and bring that pedal up to the one or two o'clock position. Now control your side-to-side balance by applying pressure on the pedals and brakes and changing the angle of the front wheel, as needed. It takes practice but really comes in handy at stoplights, on switchbacks, and when trying to free a foot before falling.

Tread: The riding surface, particularly regarding singletrack.

USGS: Short for United States Geological Survey. USGS publishes high-quality topographic maps.

Water bar: A barrier, often made of logs or rocks packed over with dirt, built into the trail to divert water from the trail, thereby preventing erosion. Be careful, because if the dirt has washed away, peeled logs can be slippery and cause bad falls, especially when they angle sharply across the trail. In some state forests, DEM has built water bars out of recycled rubber flaps that fold when you ride over them.

About the Author

After living in Santa Fe and San Francisco, Anna Milkowski returned to the Berkshires, reveling in sunny, wooded trails after too many thorns and too much fog. She once worked at a bike shop in Berkshire County, advising customers of riding hotspots and racing criteriums around the store when business was slow. A stint as an ecology researcher has developed her eye for an ash, and Anna attempts to identify trees as she rides. She researched and wrote for the travel guide *Let's Go Spain* and has worked as an editorial intern at *Outside* magazine. Latest adventure: teaching high school biology.